CW0068543Ø

VICTORIANA

VICTORIANA

Arts, Letters, and Curiosities
of the Nineteenth Century

NICK LOURAS

CASTLE IMPRINT
NEW YORK
2019

Castle Imprint

www.castleimprint.com

Book design by Grzegorz Japoł

ISBN 978-1-7327399-2-5

First Edition

Contents

To Kimberly, my love.

That after men might turn the page
And light on fancies true & sweet
And kindle with a loyal heat
To fair Victoria's golden age.

—Alfred, Lord Tennyson
"To the Queen" (draft), 1851

ᏧIntroduction

The reign of Queen Victoria from 1837 to 1901 coincided with an unprecedented flourishing of invention, industry, and creativity in Britain. The transatlantic telegraph, Bessemer steel, modern sewage systems, and the first forays into analytical computing were all introduced during this time, when the British Empire governed a quarter of the globe. In the Anglosphere of the twenty-first century we have inherited the technologies of the nineteenth century but we have not inherited the culture that once contained them. The World Wars obliterated that culture. In the crisis of the early twentieth century the context in which the modern world had been developing was suddenly removed.

Was a different modernity possible? Something more romantic? Something more authentic? A future of dirigibles, telephones, monarchy, railways (instead of motorways), heritage crafts, muscular Christianity, classical education, art and architecture that continued to develop *within* the Western canon not *against* it?

The Victorian period occupies a special place in our popular culture. Every year it is recreated on page, stage, and screen in pastiche. No other era is revisited with such regularity. What is it that fascinates us? I believe we see in the Victorian past a future that might have been. *Or that might yet be.* The Victorians were forced by the exigencies of history to find a balance between tradition and innovation—hierarchy and populism—community and individuality—the old and the new. These forces coexisted, if not always comfortably, then at least sympathetically and effectively. We have lost that balance. Sooner or later the exigencies of our own history will demand that we strike it again.

This book involves a cultural history of nineteenth-century Britain. I write "a" cultural history and not "the" cultural history because it is by no means exhaustive. The major figures in arts and letters are examined in detail: Charles Dickens and the Pre-Raphaelite painters particularly. But you will read nothing of Darwin, Marx, or Freud. And you will read rather more about Thomas De Quincey and Arthur Machen than you might in another book about the period. Insomuch as I have written a general introduction to Victorian arts and letters, I have also, necessarily, written a very personal one. I trust that you will encounter in these pages interesting people and works previously unfamiliar, and familiar ones from unexpected angles. If I am successful you will come away with a touchstone to that lost future that still fascinates us. What you will make of it—indeed, what we will make of it as a society—remains to be seen.

ARTS

1
Queen Victoria
and the Arts

The Queen's Gallery at Buckingham Palace hosted a superlative exhibition in 2010, entitled, *Victoria & Albert: Art & Love.* The exhibition brought together works commissioned and collected by the royal couple. To be in the midst of a collection so vast and personal was to be brought into a sort of rare proximity to Victoria and her age. Or so it felt to me at the time as I toured the gallery with my wife. One of the revelations of this exhibition was the extent to which the royal couple not only encouraged but guided the development of British and European art in the nineteenth century.

Queen Victoria and her husband Prince Albert were enthusiastic in their patronage of the arts. The contemporary painter William Powell Frith observed that their "treatment of artists displayed a gracious kindness delightful to experience." They both had substantial training in the field. Queen Victoria had received drawing lessons for almost ten years from Richard Westall, an RA famous for his portraits of Lord Byron. She subsequently learned oil and watercolor technique from the Scottish landscape painter William Leighton Leitch, with whom she studied for over twenty years.

For his own part, Prince Albert was among the best-educated collectors of his day. As explained in the curatorial notes for *Art & Love*, His Royal Highness

> belonged to the first generation of students to hear lectures in the new discipline of Art History. Visiting Italy as a nineteen-year-old he

had steeped himself in Renaissance painting and made contact with leading scholars, many of them German expatriates. Ludwig Gruner, an engraver from Dresden famous for his prints after Raphael, became the Prince's artistic adviser in 1842. Gruner acquired for Prince Albert twenty-seven Italian pictures of the kind then known as 'Primitives'...

The Prince was an avid collector of Medieval and Renaissance art, and a champion of modern practitioners of the style, including the painter William Dyce, to whom he awarded the commission to paint the interior of the Palace of Westminster. Frith's daughter, Jane Ellen Panton, recalled that, "[Albert] honestly loved art for art's sake, and...did more for artists than any king or prince ever did before or since."

The royal couple often met artists and visited their studios in person, an unusual practice for royalty. They were known to offer frank critiques and even suggestions. Frith commented on their extensive knowledge. He was specifically impressed by Albert's ability to discuss the composition, light, and shading of a painting. Frith afterwards followed some of Albert's suggestions, as did the painter John Martin, who affirmed that they were thoughtful, valuable, and reflected well on the Prince's understanding of art.

Victoria cannily worked with Franz Xaver Winterhalter and other court painters to portray the royal family in such a way as to reflect both the Queen's political supremacy and the Prince's authority as *pater familias*. From the same curatorial notes quoted above:

> Queen Victoria was the first Queen Regnant, and Prince Albert the first male consort, since the early 1700s. This presented a challenge to portrait painters, since the conventions that had been appropriate for Victoria's male predecessors no longer applied.
>
> Winterhalter looked for inspiration to the Dutch and Flemish old masters, especially

Van Dyck, but his Royal Family in 1846 was a brilliant and original response to the challenge. The viewer is left in no doubt that the Queen and her eldest son represent the royal line, while Prince Albert rules the family.

Winterhalter's family picture quickly became famous through public exhibition and engraving.

It was not only the traditional arts which attracted royal attention and patronage. Prince Albert was interested in how art could be related to manufacturing, making practical items beautiful, and beautiful items available to a broader section of the public. He wanted to encourage the development of good taste even among those whose surroundings and possessions were primarily practical or commercial. The royal couple encouraged the development of electroplating and electroforming as well as 'Parian ware,' a type of porcelain made to imitate marble. They often allowed manufacturers to replicate items from the Royal Collection by these new methods.

In her catalogue, *Passionate Patrons*, Leah Kharibian writes that,

> art played a key role in every aspect of their daily lives. As patrons and collectors their tastes were exceptionally wide-ranging, taking in all types of art from early Renaissance panel paintings to sculpture, furniture, jewellery, miniatures, watercolours and the new art of photography. As a couple they took a keen interest in the serious endeavors of cataloguing, conserving and displaying both their new acquisitions and the magnificent inheritance of the Royal Collection. But they enjoyed themselves immensely, too. A large proportion of their purchases were bought as gifts for each other—often as surprises. They took great delight in planning and participating in magnificent balls and fancy-dress parties, musical evenings and theatrical experiences.

Victoria went to the theater or opera on thirty-six occasions during her coronation year alone, and she and Albert were patrons of both. They held many formal dances, including three costume balls. The most famous of these was a Medieval-themed ball at Buckingham Palace in 1842 to benefit the silk weavers of Spitalfields. The royal couple received guests in the Throne Room, on a raised dais under an ornate Gothic canopy, dressed as King Edward III and his consort Queen Philippa of Hainault. Their splendid costumes were based on the real tomb effigies of their predecessors.

The design and decoration of the royal residences also engaged the Queen and Prince. They expanded Buckingham Palace, adding the east wing and the Renaissance-revival ballroom. In Scotland, they erected the current Balmoral Castle, which they decorated in a fanciful Scottish vernacular, with tartan and thistles. Prince Albert contributed to the design of Osborne House on the Isle of Wight. This included a sculpture gallery and served as an important showcase for the art that they collected.

The death of Prince Albert in 1861, at the age of forty-two, was a shocking blow for the Queen personally, and for the country. He was in my opinion the greatest public servant that Britain has ever had. Queen Victoria remained in mourning until her own death in 1901. She continued to advance the artistic genres and artists that the Prince had championed, and that together they had cultivated, for the rest of her reign.

2
John Ruskin and the Arts

The art critic John Ruskin believed that "wise work" has three characteristics: it is honest, it is useful, and it is cheerful.

Ruskin studied at Oxford and toured Europe as a young man in the 1840s. He developed an admiration for the architecture of the High Middle Ages, *viz.* gothic. He determined, writes P.D. Anthony, in *John Ruskin's Labour*, "that it required forms of social organization and forms of manual labour that are superior to those of contemporary society" and "which are essential to human development and happiness." Modest masons and craftsmen working in their own limited spheres had the opportunity "to express themselves in magnificent creations which transcended the humble contributions of ordinary men."

By 1854 Ruskin was contemplating "a great work" he meant "to write on politics—founded on the thirteenth century." However Nicholas Shrimpton writes, in *The Cambridge Companion to John Ruskin*, that by the end of the decade he "had turned away from overt medievalism to a deeper, more implicit use of medieval assumptions. Pre-modern concepts, such as intrinsic value and the 'just price,' were applied to modern problems in a series of controversial books and lectures."

In the 1870s Ruskin founded the Guild of St George. Its mission was to encourage arts education, independent craftsmanship, and sustainable agriculture among the working classes. He attempted to spread the message of the guild through a series of pamphlets collectively titled, *Fors Clavigera*. Shrimpton writes, "these texts would seek to suggest an alternative to the industrialism, capitalism, and urbanization of modern society."

Ruskin's program was the inspiration for the Arts and Crafts movement developed by William Morris in the 1880s. Morris's philosophy was a somewhat uneasy amalgamation of Ruskinian and Marxist ideas. But Ruskin's own critique of *laissez-faire* came from the Right, not the Left. "I am, and my father was before me," he wrote, "a violent Tory of the old school," whose politics were marked by "a most sincere love of kings, and dislike of everybody who attempted to disobey them." He was a strict Protestant, and although he had a religious crisis in middle age, Anthony writes, his "Christian faith developed and broadened as he grew older."

From the perspective of the present day, when the interests of labor are considered the purview of the political Left, it is edifying to consider someone who devoted the whole of his considerable intellect to the welfare of the working classes, for reasons of traditionalism and *noblesse oblige*. Shrimpton traces Ruskin's thought, writing that he was not,

> an ancestor of the British Labour Party...Neither the Marxian nor the Fabian branch of English socialism was significantly Ruskinian...his politics and economics belong to a different and more marginal tradition which stretches from the Ultra-Tories and Götzists...of the 1820s and '30s, through the Tory Young Englanders of the 1840s, to the Arts and Crafts and 'back to the land' movements of the 1880s, and the Guild Socialism and Distributism of the early twentieth century, with partial echoes in some of the Green or Ecological parties of the present day.

This entire "marginal tradition" has been pushed well outside the margins of political debate in the twenty-first century. Our civic life seems poorer for that.

3
ᏟᏔhe Pre-Raphaelite ᏟᏴrotherhood

In the autumn of 1848, John Everett Millais, Dante Gabriel Rossetti, and William Holman Hunt met to discuss their common interest in art. They had already begun this dialogue as students at the Royal Academy, and as members of a sketching circle, the Cyclographic Club. Nineteen year old Millais was by far the most accomplished, having entered the Royal Academy Schools in 1840, at the age of eleven. There he earned a string of prestigious prizes. Rossetti, a year older than Millais, but lacking his precocious talent, was still developing technique. His commitment to a career in the arts was often distracted by a calling to poetry. Nevertheless he studied painting first at Sass's Academy, then at the Royal Academy, before dropping out in March of 1848, to join the atelier of Ford Madox Brown. Holman Hunt was admitted to the Royal Academy Schools in 1844 on his third attempt. There he befriended Millais and with him shared certain frustrations with the way painting was taught.

Millais and Hunt believed that English art as practiced under the auspices of the Academy was too often lax in detail, removed from nature, and clichéd in theme and composition. This they attributed to the rigid Neoclassicism of the curriculum. The Academy's late founder, Sir Joshua Reynolds had, according to Hunt, "thought it expedient to take the Italian School at its proudest climax as a starting-point for English art." Hunt believed that this focus deprived young artists of "the training that led to the making of Michelangelo." Instead of learning to draw precisely from nature, students learned to repeat certain formulas and compositions.

The method of instruction practiced at the Academy came from the Mannerists of the Italian High Renaissance who learned by copying Raphael and, in turn, systematized Raphael's intensely personal style into a school of art. Even in nineteenth century England, Raphael's dramatic poses, dynamism, elongated and simplified forms, and distorted perspective were standards of narrative painting. Millais and Hunt believed this method to be entirely artificial, producing inferior copies of copies, deprived of the genius that had animated the original.

Hunt was quick to emphasize that "Pre-Raphaelitism is not Pre-Raphaelism." The genius of Raphael himself was not in question. Nor, for that matter, was the genius of Reynolds, who had been the preeminent portrait painter of his day. Reynolds is often remembered as a *bête noir* of the Pre-Raphaelites, but their objection was more to his pedagogy than his art. "The rules...which he loved so much to lay down were no fetters to him," Hunt wrote, "because he rose superior to them when his unbounded love of human nature was appealed to." What they rejected was the notion that the genius of an artist or an art form could be broken down into certain axioms or stereotypes and thus learned by rote. Hunt's criticism of Reynolds and the Royal Academy was that the "independent genius of the first President could not be transmitted, but his binding rules were handed on."

Neoclassicism had been the universal language of high art in Europe since the Renaissance. With its simplicity, grandeur, and strict geometry, it had supplanted the more personal, decorative, variegated art of the Middle Ages. Medieval art had possessed its own universal language, Gothic, but it also accommodated the vernacular. High art and low art were woven together with threads of sanctity, earthiness, Christian piety, color, abundance, light and darkness, strangeness, whimsy, mystery, transcendence. The rational, top-down, organizing principle of classicism, for all its beauty and orthodoxy, rarely acknowledged the vernacular or the local, or touched the roots of a culture. The English gardens and terraced houses of the Georgian period stand out as rare glorious examples of Neoclassical vernacular.

Writing at the end of the nineteenth century, the French

art critic Robert de la Sizeranne observed that, "Until 1848, one could admire art in England, but would not be surprised by it. Reynolds and Gainsborough were great masters, but they were eighteenth-century painters rather than eighteenth-century English painters. It was their models, their ladies and young girls, rather than brushwork, which gave an English character to their creations." In looking back to an earlier art form it is clear that the Pre-Raphaelites were seeking a technique and aesthetic that would give expression to the English imagination. Hunt was unequivocal in later life, writing, "every student of art in past was loyal to his own nationality, and that in these days men of British blood, whether of insular birth or of the homes beyond the seas, should not subject themselves to the influence of masters alien to the sentiments and principles of the great English poets and thinkers." It was Rossetti more than either of the other founders of the Pre-Raphaelite movement who advanced Medievalism as the vehicle for a national arts.

In 1847 Holman Hunt had his painting *The Eve of St Agnes* accepted by the jury for the Royal Academy Exhibition. At the show, Rossetti approached him, as Hunt later recalled, "repeating with emphasis his praise, and loudly declaring that my picture . . . was the best in the collection. Probably the fact that the subject was taken from Keats made him the more unrestrained, for I think no one had ever before painted any subject from this still little-known poet." Hunt invited Rossetti to his studio where Hunt showed him his latest paintings and drawings. "I rejoiced to display [them] before a man of his poetic instincts," Hunt wrote, "and it was pleasant to hear him repeat my propositions and theories in his own richer phrase." He showed Rossetti a painting inspired by Edward Bulwer-Lytton's novel *Rienzi* in which Hunt was "putting in practice the principle of rejection of conventional dogma, and pursuing that of direct application to Nature for each feature."

The seeds of the Pre-Raphaelite aesthetic were thus established before the three artists decided to form a group. To their first meeting they invited the writer William Michael Rossetti, Dante's younger brother, who was to be the chronicler and organizer of the group; Thomas Woolner, a sculptor; and the painters James Collinson and Frederic G. Stephens. It is unknown if the seven young men attempted to establish a credo or manifesto at their first meeting. They did produce a broad statement of principles:

1. To have genuine ideas to express.
2. To study nature attentively, so as to know how to express them.
3. To sympathize with what is direct and serious and heartfelt in previous art, to the exclusion of what is conventional and self-parading and learned by rote.
4. And most indispensable of all, to produce thoroughly good pictures and statues.

This rather vague manifesto suggests that at the beginning the Pre-Raphaelite Brotherhood lacked a uniform direction. The members had diverse approaches to art, varying depths of familiarity with art history, and unequal technical skills. They all, as William Rossetti noted, "belonged to the middle or lower-middle class of society." None of them with the exception of William and Dante Rossetti had the kind of liberal education which included the study of Latin and Greek. During their monthly meetings, which were held with some regularity from late 1848 to the middle of 1850, they discussed their opinions on art with as much clarity as could be expected from individuals who were then just beginning to frame the general outlines of their practices. The most voluble of the three principle members, and the most adept at formulating his ideas, was Dante Gabriel Rossetti. He had, so his brother recalled, "an abundance of ideas, pictorial and also literary, and was fuller of 'notions' than" Millais or Hunt, with a "turn for proselytizing and 'pronunciamentos.'" He was the most defiant of the group, according to William, and, with a kind of adolescent verve, he held "art-sympathies highly developed in one direction, and unduly or even ignorantly restricted in others."

At the first meeting of the Brotherhood, Millais exhibited a book of engravings that he kept in his studio. It contained poorly drawn reproductions of the frescoes at the Campo Santo in Pisa. Despite their limitations the engravings allowed the young artists to acquire some knowledge of fourteenth century Italian painting. This they supplemented with trips to the National Gallery, to view its collection of thirteenth and fourteenth century paintings, and no doubt by reading Anna Brownell Jameson's *Memoirs of the Early Italian Painters*, recently published in 1845.

Another volume that Millais shared with his colleagues was perhaps even more important to their project. This was a book of engravings by Joseph Ritter von Führich, illustrating the dramatic poem, *Life and Death of Saint Genevieve*, by the German Romantic poet, Ludwig Tieck. The Medieval style and themes would have stirred the interest of all who attended the meeting. Von Führich was a member of a group of German painters who styled themselves, the Brotherhood of St Luke. They were known also as the Nazarenes. They established themselves in Rome in 1810, where, dressed in biblical costume, the "brothers" lived communally in an abandoned monastery. Like the nascent Pre-Raphaelite Brotherhood they abandoned Neoclassicism for the spiritual values and aesthetics of the Late Middle Ages and the early Renaissance. Although the Pre-Raphaelites did not formally pattern themselves after the Nazarenes, the influence of the latter on the former is visible in early Pre-Raphaelite drawings. Examples of this influence can be seen in Millais's *Two Lovers by a Rose Bush*, and Rossetti's drawing, *The First Anniversary of the Death of Beatrice.*

The three principle members of the newly formed Brotherhood began to prepare works for exhibition in 1849, Millais and Hunt at the Royal Academy, Rossetti at the Free Exhibition. Rossetti chose as his subject *The Girlhood of Mary the Virgin*. None of the young artists had sufficient funds to hire models at this point so Rossetti turned to his mother, Frances, and sister, Christina, to sit for St Anne and the Virgin, respectively. They modeled for him periodically at Holman Hunt's studio, which Rossetti shared. This working arrangement was fruitful, though it necessitated some measure of compromise. Hunt liked people around and Rossetti preferred solitude. Both profited from discussions on art and pursued their goals independently.

For his piece, Hunt completed the scene from Bulwer-Lytton that he had earlier previewed for Rossetti, titled, *Rienzi vowing to obtain justice for the death of his young brother, slain in a skirmish between the Colonna and the Orsini factions.* Hunt's composition followed a tradition of heroic battlefield death scenes established in the eighteenth century by Benjamin West in his *Death of General Wolfe.*

Millais was the second of the group to try his hand at illustrating a scene from the poetry of John Keats. His painting, *Lorenzo and Isabella,* was an adaptation of Keats's poem *Isabella, or the Pot of Basil,* itself an adaptation of a story from Boccaccio's *Decameron.* Both poems concern a young woman from a wealthy family, Isabella, who falls in love with one of her brothers' retainers, Lorenzo. Her brothers, who plan to marry her to a rich man, learn of the romance. They lure the hapless Lorenzo to an out-of-the-way place, and there, murder him. Lorenzo appears to Isabella in a dream and leads her to his body. She digs it up and cuts off the head, which she plants in a pot of basil. Watered by her tears, the plant thrives. Her brothers grow suspicious and steal the pot, only to discover the rotting head of their victim within it. Horrified by what they have done the brothers leave Florence in self-imposed exile. Isabella, having lost both her lover and the solace of the pot of basil, descends into madness and dies.

For his painting, Millais chose to depict the moment that the brothers become aware of the romance. The scene is set around a table, at which Isabella, her brothers, and their guests are dining. Lorenzo is seated beside Isabella. He offers her a blood orange, cut in half, as if to foreshadow his own severed head, while the brothers watch from across the table. There are two focal points in the composition. The first is the young couple: Lorenzo, bowing to offer his plate, regarding his lover with gentle, even reverential, concern, but also conspiracy, and the hardness of resolve; Isabella, accepting the orange, but looking down, aware of the danger, resisting the urge to acknowledge him, her body tense with the effort of self-denial. The other focal point is one of her brothers, seated in the foreground, across from them. He is an extraordinary, brutish character, leaning forward to kick a dog who cowers in Isabella's lap. In an outstretched hand he cracks a nut with a levered nutcracker.

Curator Carol Jacobi, in a 2012 essay on the painting,

draws attention to a shadow cast on the table by the brother's arm. It appears to rise diagonally from his groin in the place of a phallus. Jacobi connects this to the "salt cellar spilling its contents," which, together with the "shadow and groin," she describes as "an unambiguous equivalent for ejaculation." Millais has created a sort of moral manifesto, contrasting these two models of manhood: the chaste, modest, chivalrous Lorenzo with the vulgar, murderous, and sexually incontinent brother.

All three paintings revealed a Medieval influence, whether in subject matter (Hunt's *Rienzi*), style (Rossetti's *Virgin*), or both (Millais's *Isabella*). Rossetti in particular captured elements reminiscent of an altarpiece in his domestic scene. Despite the ambiguousness of their initial statement, the clear meaning of the Brotherhood's name was reflected in each contribution.

The initials P.R.B. appended to the signatures of Millais, Hunt, and Rossetti, apparently went unnoticed on the paintings they exhibited at the Royal Academy and elsewhere in 1849. This was not the case the following year when they caught the attention of Charles Dickens. The meaning of the enigmatic letters had been revealed to the public before the opening of the Royal Academy show. On May 4, 1850 a columnist wrote in *The Illustrated London News*, that for those confused by the letters P.R.B., the secret was that they stood for the Pre-Raphaelite Brotherhood, a group of "ingenious gentlemen who profess themselves practitioners of Early Christian Art." Dickens wrote a scathing critique of the Pre-Raphaelite paintings for his journal, *Household Words*. In the edition of June 15, 1850, Dickens began his review of the annual Royal Academy show with a warning: "You will have the goodness to discharge from your minds all *Post*-Raphael ideas, all religious aspirations, all elevating thoughts, all tender, awful, sorrowful, ennobling, sacred, graceful, or beautiful associations, and to prepare yourselves...for the lowest depths of what is mean, odious, repulsive, and revolting."

The target of this criticism was a painting by Millais, *Christ in the House of His Parents*. As the title suggests, the work depicts a scene from the boyhood of Jesus. The setting is Saint Joseph's workshop, which Millais based on a real carpenter's shop on Oxford Street in London. The composition is rich in Christian symbolism. Jesus has cut His hand on a nail. Blood runs from the center of His palm to the foot beneath it, prefiguring the wounds of the crucifixion. The Virgin Mary kneels before Him, as though at the foot of the cross. A young John the Baptist brings water to clean the wound, foreshadowing his baptism of Christ. A white dove, the symbol of the Holy Spirit, watches from a ladder in the background. A triangle on the wall above Christ's head suggests the Trinity. Outside a flock of sheep is gathered, anticipating His mission as shepherd of men.

If Dickens saw any of this he did not recognize it. He accused Millais of portraying the savior as "a hideous, wry-necked, blubbering, red-headed boy," and the Virgin Mary as a "Monster" who would stand out "in her ugliness" from the company of "the vilest cabaret in France, or the lowest ginshop in England." Sweeping the rest of the company into his critique, he wrote, "Wherever it is possible to express ugliness of feature, limb, or attitude, you have it expressed."

When we look at the painting today we see none of the depravity that Dickens portrays. The religious subject is treated with reverence. The figures are rendered with great tenderness. The naturalism, though striking, was hardly novel, having a precedence going back to Caravaggio. What could possibly have elicited such contempt?

Dickens was clearly reacting to something other than the technical merits of the painting when he wrote his review. We do not have to search far to learn what that was: Dickens found the notion of a backward-looking movement plainly offensive. He compared the Pre-Raphaelite Brotherhood to a hypothetical "Pre-Newtonian Brotherhood" for those who objected to being bound by the laws of gravity, a "Pre-Galileo Brotherhood" for those who "refuse[d] to perform any annual revolution round the Sun," a "Pre-Gower and Pre-Chaucer Brotherhood" for those who would revive the old idiosyncratic English spellings, or a "Pre-Laurentians Brotherhood" for those who would abolish printed books in favor of painstakingly copied manuscripts.

The progressive outlook which dominated liberal thought in the Victorian period, as it does today, held that the arrow of time moves only and ever forward toward a distant perfection of human society. The suggestion that we might restore modes of life from the past threatened the idealism that underpinned so many of the endeavors of nineteenth-century modernity. A progressive like Dickens would have understood the conservative implications of Pre-Raphaelitism perhaps better than the young artists themselves.

Holman Hunt's contribution to the Royal Academy exhibition was intended as a companion piece to Millais's, and was, in composition, even more ambitious. The subject, and title, was, *A Converted British Family Sheltering a Christian Missionary from the Persecution of the Druids*. In the foreground Hunt depicted the interior of a simple wooden fisherman's shed on a riverbank, where the titular missionary has collapsed into the arms of the mother of the family, while the men guard the door, and the children succor him. In the background, seen in part through the windows at the top of the hut, a mob of pagans, commanded by a Druid priest, chase down a second missionary to his inevitable martyrdom. Although the scene has its own dramatic narrative and tension, Hunt's composition suggests an episode from the Gospels: the Deposition of Christ, when the Savior's body was lowered from the cross. Here the postures of the missionary and the woman holding him from behind clearly evoke the *Pietà*, the traditional artistic representation of Mary cradling the body of Jesus. On the wall above them is a red cross roughly drawn by the persecuted Christians for their worship. One of the daughters removes a thorn from the missionary's robe, representing the crown of thorns, while another prepares to bathe his face with sponge and water.

Exhibited together, the relationship between Hunt's painting, and Millais's *Christ in the House of His Parents*, would have been readily apparent. Both works depicted a primitive Christianity. Both employed traditional, iconographic details. In portraying scenes from Christian history before and after the crucifixion, both placed Christ's passion at the center of the narrative. Hunt judged his painting to be among the best of his own work. Appraising it more than two decades later, he wrote to Edward Lear, "sometimes when I look at the Early Xtians I feel rather ashamed that I have got no further than later years have brought me, but the truth is that at twenty—health, enthusiasm and yet unpunished confidence in oneself carries a man very near his ultimate length of tether."

Both Hunt and Rossetti had benefitted in their education from a trip to the Continent in the fall of 1849. They visited France and Belgium. In Paris they toured the large public galleries, studying canvases by Titian, da Vinci, Veronese, and van Dyck. At the Louvre they were awestruck by *The Coronation of the Virgin* by Fra Angelico, which was, according to Hunt, "of peerless grace and sweetness in the eyes of us both." In Antwerp they admired the paintings of the Early Netherlandish artists, Jan van Eyck and Hans Memling, as well as those of Rubens and van Dyck. They were prepared for their encounter with the brilliant, detailed works of the Early Netherlandish painters, having already studied van Eyck's 1434 work, *Portrait of Giovanni Arnolfini and his Wife*, at the National Gallery. It was the graphic quality, almost brittle composition, and absence of free, painterly brush strokes in the paintings by van Eyck and his followers that became the goal of Hunt and Rossetti for their own works.

Of all the paintings exhibited by members of the Brotherhood in 1850, the most influential on the development of Pre-Raphaelite style and technique, was Rossetti's *Ecce Ancilla Domini (The Annunciation)*, shown at the National Institution, formerly the Free Exhibition. The painting had begun with a preliminary sketch in late November of 1849. This process was recorded by Rossetti's brother William in his journal. He described the work-in-progress as depicting the Virgin in bed, "without any bedclothes on, an arrangement which may be justified in consideration of the hot climate, and the Angel Gabriel is to be presenting a lily to her." The painting was to be almost entirely white, with contained uses of one color at a time: a red embroidery in the foreground, a blue curtain in the background, yellow halos, a window opened on a blue sky.

In mid-December, Rossetti began to paint the Virgin's head, using his sister Christina as a model, and later in the month drew the head of the Angel, with his brother William modeling. By mid-January he was busy working on the drapery and in early February had moved on to the red cloth embroidery in the foreground. On March 29, William recorded that his brother had painted the feet and arm of the Angel from a model, had another,

Miss Love, sit for the Virgin's hair, and a third to finish the Angel's head. The execution was a protracted process as Rossetti, now working in the studio of Ford Madox Brown, struggled to achieve the level of technical mastery possessed by his colleagues. The finished product was a painting of exceptional tenderness and beauty, in some ways less mature that Hunt's or Millais's work, but in others, particularly the figure of the Virgin, entirely developed.

With this painting Rossetti introduced what would become a signature Pre-Raphaelite technique. Whereas most artists prepared their canvases with a coat of neutral, solid color, called a toned ground, Rossetti painted his canvas bright white. As one modern curator writes, "The particularly luminous white ground...made the pure colors brushed over it seem illuminated." Beginning in 1850 both Millais and Hunt adopted this practice, amplifying the effect by using a *wet* white ground. Millais used the technique to depict sunlight on faces in his painting, *The Woodsman's Daughter*, completed the following year. Its application can be seen to great advantage in Hunt's adaptation of Shakespeare's *Two Gentlemen of Verona*, titled, *Valentine Rescuing Sylvia from Proteus*, also completed in 1851. In this painting particularly, Hunt achieved what has been described as "an almost preternatural luminosity."

Experimentation with color had been an ongoing interest of all three artists. Hunt recalled a visit to the Royal Academy by the painter Claude Lorraine Nursey during one of Hunt's first terms there. Nursey had given a lecture and then stayed to watch the students work. At the time Hunt was copying Sir David Wilkie's painting, *The Blind Fiddler*. Nursey had once been a pupil of Wilkie and explained the latter's practice of applying all his paint, whether for a section of a painting or an entire work, in one sitting. In this way he never painted over dried paint, as most artists did, which tended to dull the colors. For Hunt this had been a revelation. "I tried the method," he wrote, "and I now looked at all paintings with the question whether they had been so executed. I began to trace the purity of work in the quattrocentists to the drilling of undeviating manipulation with which fresco-painting had furnished them, and I tried to put aside the loose, irresponsible handling to which I had been trained, and which was nearly universal at the time, and to adopt the practice which excused no false touch." Hunt seems to have arrived at the technique that he used in *Valentine Rescuing Sylvia* by combining the innovations of Rossetti and Wilkie. By painting on a *wet* white ground he was able to achieve more luminous colors even than Rossetti had, but only because he had rigorously adopted Wilkie's constraints. As Hunt observed, "Painting of this kind cannot be retouched except with an entire loss of luminosity."

Millais had been experimenting with similar methods around this same time. Hunt remembered both Millais and himself arriving at the use of a wet white ground independent of one another. This would seem to suggest that the various influences that informed the technique were being discussed among the members of the Brotherhood during their meetings leading up to the various individual applications. Once it had been perfected, Millais proposed that they should keep the process "as a precious secret" amongst themselves, which they did. When Millais and Hunt revealed the secret to Ford Madox Brown, years later, Brown recognized it as a technique of the late-Medieval and early-Renaissance fresco painters. According to Hunt, Brown "enlarged on the mystery as nothing less than the secret of the old masters, who thus secured the transparency and solidity...valued so much in fresco, the wet white half dry forming an equivalent to the moist intonaco grounds upon which the master had to do his painting of that day while the surface was still humid."

While the Pre-Raphaelites worked on their paintings for the 1850 exhibition, discussion at their meetings centered around the publication of a journal, intended to circulate the ideas and aesthetics of the Brotherhood. The first issue of *The Germ* appeared on January 1, 1850. The title was an expression of the Brotherhood's commitment to the smallest detail of nature—the germ, the seed—but also of their creative aspiration: it was the germ of an idea and a movement.

The first issue contained essays; reviews; poems by Thomas Woolner, Ford Madox Brown, Dante, William, and Christina Rossetti; and an etching by Holman Hunt to illustrate Woolner's poem, "My Beautiful Lady." It is not surprising that the Rossetti siblings dominated the contents of the journal. They belonged to a multigenerational literary family of mixed English and Italian stock and were all comfortable with the practice of writing. Their father, Gabriele Pasquale Rossetti, was an exiled Sicilian Dante scholar. Their maternal uncle was John Polidori, the physician and confidante of Lord Byron. Dr Polidori had created the modern vampire genre with his short story, "The Vampyre," written in answer to a challenge from Lord Byron to compose a ghost story. That same challenge, issued to Byron's guests one evening at the Villa Diodati in Switzerland, had prompted Mary Shelley to write *Frankenstein*.

The Rossetti household revolved around the study of Dante, Petrarch, and other early Italian writers and was often full of émigré scholars. Dante Gabriel was immersed in the life of his namesake and like his father would contribute to the corpus of literature on Medieval Italian poetry. A fourth sibling, Maria, later wrote her own book on Dante.

The children had been raised in the Church of England and educated at home by their parents, learning from the Bible, St Augustine, *Pilgrim's Progress*, the English classics, pedagogical novels, and fairy tales. The bohemian family, though highly cultured, was never financially secure. When health problems forced Gabriele Rossetti to step down from his professorship at King's College in 1843, much of the burden of supporting the household fell on the children. Christina suffered bouts of depression and weak health, though she found catharsis in Christianity and in poetry. Her faith naturally permeated her writing. Biographer Lona Mosk Packer cites "the Bible, hagiographies, folk and fairy tales" as her first influences. Christina's best known poem, "In Bleak Midwinter," is sung as a Christmas carol in Anglican churches to this day.

The two poems that she contributed to *The Germ* stand out in their maturity. At this point Christina was already an accomplished poet, having published work in the *Athenaeum*. "Dream Land" contains a nimble, subtle interweaving of her influences, at once describing the enchanted slumber of a fairy tale maiden, and the soul of the sleeping dead, awaiting the resurrection of the body. In this, her verse achieves a melancholy beauty:

> Rest, rest, a perfect rest,
> Shed over brow and breast;
> Her face is toward the west,
> The purple land.
> She cannot see the grain
> Ripening on hill and plain;
> She cannot feel the rain
> Upon her hand.

The sadness that permeates her early poems no doubt reflected the emotional turmoil that Christina was then undergoing, though it was also perfectly characteristic of Victorian late-romantic verse. Her second contribution to the inaugural issue of *The Germ*, titled, "An End," is no less mournful.

In reading through the four numbers of *The Germ* one is struck by the consistency of approach and subject matter in the poetry. The verse represents an extension of the discussions engaged in by the artists at their meetings and of the paintings they were producing.

James Collinson wrote a long poem, "The Child Jesus," published in the second number. It was influenced by Millais' picture, *Christ in the House of His Parents*. Collinson's description of the cottages overlooking the sea in Nazareth where the Holy Family lived is quite lovely:

> A honeysuckle and a moss-rose grew,
> With many blossoms, on their cottage front;
> And o'er the gable warmed by the South
> A sunny grape vine broadened shady leaves
> Which gave its tendrils shelter, as they hung
> Trembling upon the bloom of purple fruit.

In the same issue, the poem "Morning Sleep," by William Bell Scott, art teacher and friend of Dante Gabriel Rossetti, combines images of nature with Arthurian legend. When the contribution was submitted, William Rossetti described it as "gloriously fine." Scott writes,

> The spell
> Of Merlin old that ministered to fate,

The tales of visiting ghosts, or fairy elves,
Or witchcraft, are no fables. But his task
Is ended with the night;—the thin white moon
Evades the eye, the sun breaks through the trees,
And the charmed wizard comes forth a mere man
From out his circle.

The Germ was not a success in its own time. Only 70 copies from an initial print run of 700 were sold. There were fewer readers of the second issue published on January 30, and still fewer for the third and fourth, published in March and April, respectively. The expenses of this venture were too onerous for the ambitious, though virtually penniless, artists to bear, and the support of their better-heeled friends was soon exhausted. After four issues the enterprise folded. Although *The Germ* was not a breakthrough for the Brotherhood it remains a vital record of its ideas in their earliest phase, and was reprinted several times beginning in the late nineteenth century, when the artists had achieved greater fame.

The subject matter of the Pre-Raphaelite pictures varied from artist to artist but clear commonalities were visible by the time they submitted their works for exhibition in 1851.

In addition to shared techniques, the artists shared a preference, though not exclusive, for Biblical and Medieval themes over classical and mythological, for character and mise-en-scène over landscape, and for bright color over the popular preference for smoky browns. Within this broad consensus was a great range of influences. Rossetti was particularly fascinated with Dante and Medieval devotional art; Holman Hunt with Biblical themes; Millais was more or less encyclopaedic in his references, sometimes turning to Shakespeare, at other times contemporary daily life, the Bible, English history, or contemporary Regency and Victorian poetry.

Millais produced three pictures for the Royal Academy show in 1851: *Mariana*, *The Return of the Dove to the Arc*, and *The Woodsman's Daughter*. The first was taken from a poem by Alfred, Lord Tennyson based on Shakespeare's *Measure for Measure*. In Millais's rendering, the character of Mariana looks plaintively out of large Gothic windows. She has been rejected as a bride because of the loss of her dowry in a shipwreck. The caption to the picture is from Tennyson's 1830 poem: She only said, "'My life is dreary, / He cometh not,' she said; / She said, 'I am aweary, aweary, / I would that I were dead!'"

Tennyson was a particular favorite of the Pre-Raphaelites. Undoubtedly the finest English poet of his generation, Tennyson had been appointed Poet Laureate in 1850, with the support of Prince Albert, an early admirer. The same year Tennyson published "In Memoriam," a tribute to his late friend Arthur Henry Hallam. The work was a sensation. William Rossetti, as a reviewer for *The Spectator*, received an advance copy. Upon reading it he rushed home and passed the book to his brother. Although it was after midnight Dante read the entire poem aloud. Thereafter the Pre-Raphaelites hung on Tennyson's every word, illustrating many of his works, most notably episodes from his Arthurian cycle, *Idylls of the King*.

All three of Millais's pictures in the Royal Academy show of 1851 were accomplished with deftness of drawing, flatness of surface, and minimal use of modeling in the three dimensional forms. The same may be said of Holman Hunt's submission, *Valentine Rescuing Sylvia from Proteus*. Hunt drew his subject from the climax of *Two Gentlemen of Verona*. In Shakespeare's early comedy, Valentine and Proteus both love Silvia, though her heart belongs to Valentine. After rescuing her from outlaws, Proteus threatens to rape Silvia, if she will not consent to love him. Valentine intervenes. Proteus repents and gives his love to Julia who has disguised herself as his page boy.

Reviewing Hunt's adaptation for *The Spectator*, the Rossetti brothers were, of course, effusive, calling it, "the finest we have seen from its painter." Dante drew the reader's attention to the two female figures. Silvia, he wrote, "nestles to her strong knight, rescued and secure; while poor Julia leans, sick to swooning, against a tree, and tries with a trembling hand to draw the ring from her finger. Both these figures are truly creations, for the very reason that they are appropriate individualities, and not self-seeking idealisms." William used much of the column to rebuke the hanging committee of the Royal Academy for its poor job in highlighting such an important work.

The paintings of the Pre-Raphaelites and their

associates at the Royal Academy show of 1851 received largely negative reviews. The critic of *The Times* condemned them for "the puerility or infancy of their art," their "monkish style" and "monkish follies." A "morbid infatuation" with ancient art, had, he wrote, caused them to sacrifice "truth, beauty, and genuine feeling to mere eccentricity." Clearly Charles Dickens had set the tone and terms of public debate in his review of the previous year. Detractors of the new movement shared a common rhetoric and a few common points of opposition.

The seemingly impenetrable wall of critical resistance to the Pre-Raphaelite Brotherhood would soon break, however, with the emergence of an extraordinary ally. John Ruskin was by this time a formidable art critic whose opinions held great weight among both scholars and collectors. The first two volumes of his monumental work, *Modern Painters*, had been published between 1843 and 1846. In them, Ruskin laid the philosophical groundwork for an art closer to nature. He idealized late-Medieval and Renaissance art in terms of the convergence of truth, beauty, and religion. Ruskin argued that the job of the artist was to convey "truth to nature," by which he meant "moral as well as material truth." By this measure he judged the contemporary landscape painter J.M.W. Turner to be the greatest artist who ever worked in that field, elevating him above the Old Masters of the Baroque period. He was deeply critical of the contemporary historical painters who, he wrote, were "permitted to pander more fatally every year to the vicious English taste, which can enjoy nothing but what is theatrical, entirely unchastised, nay, encouraged and lauded by the very men who endeavor to hamper our great landscape painters with rules derived from consecrated blunders." Here was the very language that the young Pre-Raphaelites were using to articulate their dissatisfaction with the prevailing wisdom of the Academy. If anyone could understand the aims of the Brotherhood, they had to hope it would be Ruskin. Indeed, his defense, when it came, was swift, authoritative, and generous.

On May 13, 1851, *The Times* published a signed letter from Ruskin expressing "regret" that the "tone" of the paper's critique of the Pre-Raphaelite paintings had been "scornful as well as severe." He wrote that the "labour bestowed on those works, and their fidelity to a certain order of truth (labour and fidelity which are altogether indisputable) ought at once to have placed them above the level of mere contempt." He insisted that the young artists were "at a turning point, from which they may either sink into nothingness or rise to very real greatness." On May 30, Ruskin followed up with a second letter, in which he concluded that the Pre-Raphaelites, "may, as they gain experience, lay in our land the foundations of a school of art nobler than has been seen for three hundred years." With these words the fortunes of the members of the Brotherhood changed forever.

The Pre-Raphaelites were emerging as integral drivers of the Medieval artistic revival that would come to define the Victorian age, largely thanks to the advocacy of two men: Ruskin and His Royal Highness Prince Albert.

The same year that Ruskin penned his defense of the Pre-Raphaelites he published the first volume in his magisterial study of Venetian Gothic architecture, *The Stones of Venice*. Here he began to lay out a philosophy of Gothicism over and against the prevailing classicism. In subsequent volumes he would elaborate on this philosophy, defining six characteristic elements of Gothic design: savageness, changefulness, naturalism, grotesqueness, rigidity, and redundance. Ruskin wrote with irresistible enthusiasm, praising Gothic ornament for its "prickly independence, and frosty fortitude, jutting into crockets, and freezing into pinnacles; here starting up into a monster, there germinating into a blossom; anon knitting itself into a branch, alternately thorny, bossy, and bristly, or writhed into every form of nervous entanglement; but even when most graceful, never for an instant languid, always quickset; erring, if at all, ever on the side of brusquerie." This was not the language of archeology. Ruskin was not describing relics or museum pieces. In his poetic prose he conjured a vital, living, irrepressible, even inevitable art form.

No one did more to midwife that art form than Prince Albert. When he married Queen Victoria in 1840 the young German prince became an influential patron and advocate for the arts in Britain. One of his first official duties was to lead the Royal Commission tasked with designing the interior of the new

Houses of Parliament. He brought to this appointment a vision entirely sympathetic with the Gothic Berry-Pugin architecture. The Prince possessed an informed taste for Medieval and Medieval-revival aesthetics. In his Lutheran culture Medieval forms had been preserved from both iconoclasm and the gaudy Baroque influence of the Counter-Reformation. He collected everything from Tuscan *trecento* primitives to contemporary German romantic painters. Under his guidance, Clare Willsdon writes, "the wall-painting, sculpture, and stained glass used as a matter of course by the medieval builders" were adopted for the new building. Prince Albert advised the artist William Dyce to draw from Arthurian legend for the murals of the Queen's Robing Room.

To a certain extent the Prince became involved in arts and culture because he lacked a formal outlet for his talents. Parliament had been opposed to granting any political power to a foreign prince. Not only was he denied the title of King Consort, he was also denied peerage and military rank. Although in time he did take on responsibility for the affairs of state, it is a credit to his genius that, for most of his short career, he had a greater influence on British culture than any other man of his age, despite having little practical power.

Beginning in 1850, the Prince, together with members of the Royal Society for the Encouragement of Arts, Manufactures, and Commerce, organized what would be the first World's Fair. The Great Exhibition, as it was known, opened in 1851 in the Kensington district of London, housed within a custom-built "Crystal Palace" of cast-iron, steel, and glass, large enough to enclose full-grown trees. The exhibition showcased rich displays of traditional culture and ultra-modern technology side by side. Visitors encountered the Koh-i-Noor diamond from India and the Daria-i-Noor from Persia; a stuffed elephant bedecked in the livery and howdah of an Indian rajah; porcelain, tapestries, and silk from France; decorative arts, furs, sledges, and Cossack armor from Russia; an Egyptian Court with towering statues and pillars, mummies, and antiquities. At the same time they could marvel at Stevenson's hydraulic press, adding machines, a state-of-the-art printing press, folding pianos, carriages, and velocipedes.

To represent Britain in this grand evocation of the Victorian future, Prince Albert invited A.W.N. Pugin to create a Medieval Court. Pugin had previously collaborated with Sir Charles Berry on the Gothic Revival design of the new Houses of Parliament. He was now in the last year of his life. This would be his swan song, what Paul Atterbury called, "his final consuming project." Pugin designed stained glass, furniture, sculpture, and textiles in the Gothic Revival style. He had these fabricated by the various firms of craftsmen with whom he had long collaborated, in what Jeffrey Auerbach describes as a "preview of the team-oriented craftsmanship that would characterize William Morris's Arts and Crafts productions." The effect, in the words of one art historian, was "to create a phantasmagoric realm for spectators."

As the Pre-Raphaelites became part of a broader Gothic Revival the Brotherhood itself became somewhat redundant to their needs. The last public exhibition of their works as a group occurred in 1852. Two of Millais's pictures hung in the Royal Academy Exhibition that year: *A Huguenot* and *Ophelia*. The former depicts a young couple in France meeting in a garden during the St Bartholomew's Day massacre, when Roman Catholics killed tens of thousands of Protestant Huguenots, over several weeks in 1572. The girl is pleading with her Protestant beau to wear the armband of the Roman Catholics so that he can escape the slaughter incognito. While he holds her, gazing tenderly into her worried eyes, he gently removes the armband that she has tied around him, choosing martyrdom as a faithful Protestant over even pretended apostasy. Millais had initially sketched this scene as a simple meeting of lovers in a brick-walled garden but on the advice of Holman Hunt he added the historic context, which they took from Mayerbeer's opera *Les Hugenots*.

The wonderful, meticulously rendered flowers and foliage in the garden are typical of the kind of botanical illustration that was immensely popular, particularly among watercolorists, in the Victorian era. The most famous of these was Marian North whose skill at rendering flowers was honored with the opening of a gallery in Kew Gardens permanently dedicated to her works in 1882. Millais's passion for setting his subject in rich, verdant, floral surroundings is nowhere more apparent than in his *Ophelia*.

Head study of Elizabeth Siddal for Ophelia
by Sir John Everett Millais, 1851.

Drawn from Shakespeare's *Hamlet*, the tragic story of Ophelia was ideally tailored to fit Victorian and specifically Pre-Raphaelite sensibility. Spurned by Prince Hamlet, she has fallen into a river, while picking flowers, and as she floats away, temporarily buoyed by the air trapped in her clothing, she sings. But as her clothes become saturated, the weight of the water pulls "the poor wretch from her melodious lay" down to a muddy death. In his depiction of the scene, Millais painted flowers mentioned by Shakespeare floating downriver with Ophelia, but he added a red poppy as a symbol of sleep and death. Millais based his gorgeously overgrown riverbank on the Hogsmill River in Surrey where he painted for several hours a day, six days a week, for five months to capture the background. In the end he had to work inside a kind of duck blind to protect himself from the cold weather.

Millais finished the painting over the winter at his studio on Gower Street in London. He based the figure of Ophelia on the newly discovered model Elizabeth Siddal, who would go on to sit for, and later marry Dante Gabriel Rossetti. She would also become an artist in her own right. *Ophelia* remains one of the most iconic of all the Pre-Raphaelite paintings. It hangs today in the Tate Britain in London and must be seen in person to be fully appreciated. Even the most detailed reproduction does not convey the awesome effect of glittering light captured by Millais, in particular where the lace of Ophelia's dress floats on the surface of the water.

Holman Hunt's painting for the 1852 exhibition was *The Hireling Shepherd*. Its subject was the neglect of duty, in this case by the titular shepherd, who ignores his flock to woo a pretty red-haired maid, showing her a death's head hawkmoth. Hunt meant to symbolize the retreat of churchmen into theological debate while their flocks were led astray for lack of moral guidance. The title is a reference to the Biblical allegory of the Good Shepherd. Hunt achieved considerable success with this painting as it was awarded a prize when exhibited at Birmingham in 1853 and sold to a collector for 120 pounds. Hunt later observed that with Millais' picture of the Hugenots also winning a prize at an exhibition in Liverpool, "the double success of our School . . . [indicated that] the recognition of our claims was thus proved to be growing."

After the amicable dissolution of the Pre-Raphaelite Brotherhood, the three artists who had been the primary force behind it, continued to discuss art with each other and to explore common aesthetics, but they pursued their careers separately. They began to inspire a number of other artists. These included Edward Burne-Jones, Arthur Hughes, William Morris, the photographer Julia Margaret Cameron, Frederick Leighton, Frank Dicksee, Frederick Sandys, Lawrence Alma-Tadema, Simeon Solomon, and John William Waterhouse, among others.

The Pre-Raphaelite conquest of the Victorian and Edwardian art world was eventually formalized with honors. Millais and Burne-Jones were given baronetcies; Leighton was given a barony; Holman Hunt received the Order of Merit as a personal gift from King Edward VII; Dicksee and Alma-Tadema were knighted.

In fact, there had long been affection for the Pre-Raphaelites at the palace. In the midst of the early controversy surrounding Millais's *Christ in the House of His Parents*, Queen Victoria had arranged for the painting to be shown privately for her at Windsor Castle. This was unprecedented. "I hope that it will not have any bad effects upon the Queen's mind," Millais joked nervously to Hunt. Gordon Fleming in his biography of Millais suggests that it did not. The following year Prince Albert gave a speech to the Royal Academy in which he reminded the members of their obligation to encourage developing artists in terms unmistakably similar to Ruskin's defense of Millais.

A more private, but in its own way equally revealing, embrace of the Pre-Raphaelites came earlier, in 1855. In January of that year, Millais and Charles Dickens met for the first time at a dinner party given by their mutual friend, Wilkie Collins. After dinner they had a long conversation. The following day, Dickens wrote Millais a letter, and sent it, along with an article from *Household Words*, about the London fire brigade, which was the subject of Millais's work-in-progress, *The Rescue*. The letter read:

> If you have in your mind any previous association with the pages in which [the article] appears (very likely you have none) it may be a rather disagreeable one. In that case I hope a word, frankly said, may make it pleasanter. Objecting very strongly to what I believed to be an unworthy use of your great powers, I once expressed the objection in this same journal. My opinion on that point is not in the least changed, but it has never dashed my admiration of your progress in what I suppose are higher and better things. In short, you have given me such great

reasons (in your works) to separate you from uncongenial association, that I wish to give you in return one little reason for doing the like by me.

Millais accepted the olive branch. Thereafter they became true friends. When Dickens died in 1870 it was Millais who was summoned to his death bed to draw the final portrait of the great author.

4
Henry James
and the Pre-Raphaelites

In 2017 I attended an exhibition on the life and work of the American novelist Henry James at the Morgan Library in New York. This was the sort of show that the Morgan does best: manuscripts, early editions, letters, portraits, along with paintings by period artists. One item in particular caught my attention for its connection to the Pre-Raphaelites. It was a letter that James wrote to his friend, the artist John La Farge. In it he describes a visit to the home of Dante Gabriel Rossetti.

A Bostonian by birth, Henry James came to England in early 1869. He would remain there for the rest of his life, being naturalized as a British subject in 1915. He was introduced to Rossetti a few months after his arrival in London by their mutual friend Charles Norton. James admired the Pre-Raphaelites and had already visited the studios of several related artists. He assessed Rossetti's work in perceptive but also candid and amusing terms in the letter to La Farge, dated June of 1869. It reads:

> I did see Rossetti, Chas. Norton having conducted me to his studio—in the most delicious melancholy old house at Chelsea on the river. When I think what Englishmen ought to be, with such homes & haunts! Rossetti however, does not shame his advantages. Personally, he struck me as unattractive—poor man, I suppose he was horribly bored!—but his pictures, as I

saw them in his room, I think decidedly strong. They were all large fanciful portraits of women, of the type *que vous savez*, narrow, special, monotonous, but with lots of beauty & power. His chief inspiration & constant model is Mrs. Wm. Morris, whom I had seen, a woman of extraordinary beauty of a certain sort—a face, in fact quite made to his hand. He has painted a dozen portraits of her—one, in particular, in a blue gown, with her hair down, pressing a lot of lilies against her breast—an almost great work.

Rossetti's "most delicious melancholy old house" was located at 16 Cheyne Walk where it still stands today. He had moved there in 1862. An 1882 watercolor by Henry Treffry Dunn offers a glimpse of the interior at the time: sea-green walls and upholstery; piles of lush Persian rugs; Delft tiles around the fireplace; paintings, mirrors, and religious icons in gilt frames on the walls. At this point Rossetti was at the height of his talents. He would spend the next decade painting what were arguably the definitive expressions of the Pre-Raphaelite style: lush, detailed, accomplished works.

The crisis of Rossetti's career—a passionate but ill-fated marriage to model and fellow artist Elizabeth Siddal—was over. The ending had been most tragic. On a February evening in 1860 he returned home to find his wife comatose from an overdose of laudanum. Though Rossetti called several physicians, they could do nothing, and she died the next morning. It may have been a deliberate suicide. William Bell Scott wrote that she had "pinned a written statement on the breast of her night-shirt and put an end to her troubles, real or imaginary." The note was supposedly taken off of her by Rossetti and destroyed by Ford Madox Brown. None of that can be proved.

Rossetti buried Lizzie with the manuscripts of his unpublished poetry sealed in her coffin. This romantic gesture came to a ghoulish end, however. He later ordered her body exhumed to retrieve the poems. Afterward, he wrote to Algernon Swinburne:

I want to tell you something lest you should hear it first from any one else. It is that I have recovered my old book of poems. Friends had long hinted such a possibility to me but it was only just lately I made up my mind to it. I hope you will think none the worse of my feeling for the memory of one for whom I know you had a true regard. The truth is, that no one so much as herself would have approved of my doing this...Art was the only thing which she felt very seriously. Had it been possible to her, I should have found the book on my pillow the night she was buried; and could she have opened the grave, no other hand would have been needed.

Lizzie influenced the aesthetic of the "Pre-Raphaelite Woman" with her red hair and pale skin. William Rossetti characterized her as "a most beautiful creature with an air between dignity and greatness." He described her as "tall, finely formed with a lofty neck and regular yet somewhat uncommon features." She had "greenish-blue unsparkling eyes, brilliant complexion and a lavish heavy wealth of copper-golden hair." Georgiana Burne-Jones, the wife of artist Edward Burne-Jones, wrote of Siddal's "beautiful deep-red hair," and her complexion, which looked "as if a rose tint lay beneath the white skin, producing a most soft and delicate pink."

Rossetti's best painting of her was done from memory and sketch studies after her death. *Beata Beatrix* represents Beatrice Portinari, the subject of Dante Alighieri's courtly love poem, *La Vita Nuova.* Lizzie-as-Beatrice is portrayed transfigured in prayer at the moment before her death. The painting connects Rossetti's own love for Lizzie with his namesake's grieving love for Beatrice. It is a subject rich in spiritual connotations. Beatrice reappears in the *Divine Comedy* as Dante's guide into Paradise.

For all of that influence, I agree with Henry James that it was Jane Morris—and I would add, Alexa Wilding—who were Rossetti's indispensible muses. At the very least they complimented a more mature talent and style than Rossetti possessed during Lizzie's lifetime. Not surprisingly the image of Jane Morris made the strongest impression on Henry James during his visit to 16 Cheyne Walk. He had met her in the flesh several months earlier in the company of her husband the artist William Morris. James described her in positively rapturous terms in a letter to his sister Alice dated March of 1869:

The Roseleaf (Portrait of Jane Morris) by Dante Gabriel Rossetti, 1870.

> *Je n'en reviens pas*—she haunts me still. A figure cut out of a missal—out of one of Rossetti's or Hunt's pictures—to say this gives but a faint idea of her, because when such an image puts on flesh and blood, it is an apparition of fearful and wonderful intensity. It's hard to say [whether]

she's a grand synthesis of all the pre-Raphaelite pictures ever made—or they a 'keen analysis' of her—whether she's an original or a copy. In either case she is a wonder. Imagine a tall lean woman in a long dress of some dead purple stuff, guiltless of hoops (or of anything else, I should say) with a mass of crisp black hair heaped into great wavy projections on each of her temples, a thin pale face, a pair of strange, sad, deep, dark Swinburnish eyes, with great thick black oblique brows, joined in the middle and tucking themselves under her hair, a mouth like 'Oriana' in our illustrated Tennyson, a long neck, without any collar, and in lieu thereof some dozen strings of outlandish beads—in fine Complete. On the wall was a large nearly full-length portrait of her by Rossetti, so strange and unreal that if you hadn't seen her, you'd pronounce it a distempered vision, but in fact an extremely good likeness.

James seems to sense the sexual magnetism between artist and model. By all accounts Rossetti and Jane Morris carried on a long affair during her marriage to the painfully un-sexual Morris. This was made all the more awkward by the fact that Rossetti lived with the Morrises for months at a time at Kelmscott Manor in Oxfordshire where he and William were artistic collaborators. Whether out of misguided hero-worship for Rossetti, or some perverse tenet of socialism (Morris wrote a utopian novel that imagined a world without marriage), Morris suffered to live with this arrangement. To his credit he seems finally to have stood up for himself. In July of 1874 Rossetti left Kelmscott suddenly, never to return.

5
The Waterhouse Muse

John William Waterhouse was the last artist to make use of the Pre-Raphaelite style in direct continuity with the first generation of Pre-Raphaelite painters. He was not strictly a Pre-Raphaelite. His interest in classical and mythological subjects placed him, with Sir Lawrence Alma-Tadema, somewhat out of the mainstream of the genre, and closer to traditional Romanticism. However a series of Arthurian, Shakespearian, and Christian paintings completed in the 1890s are boldly Pre-Raphaelite in style.

Beginning in the 1890s, and continuing until his death in 1917, Waterhouse worked primarily with one female model. Her likeness appears in his most famous works: *La Belle Dame sans Merci* (1893); *A Naiad, or Hylas with a Nymph* (1893); *Ophelia* (1894); *The Mermaid* (1901); and *Tristan and Isolde* (1914). In perhaps his most famous painting, *Hylas and the Nymphs* (1896), she appears duplicated as multiple figures.

For many years there was a mystery surrounding the identity of this model. "Who was she?" Christopher Wood asked in his 1981 book, *The Pre-Raphaelites.* "One cannot help speculating about the identity of the mysterious and beautiful model who reappears so often in...Waterhouse's pictures...It remains one of the few Pre-Raphaelite mysteries, and one that will probably never be solved."

The "Waterhouse Girl," as she was long known, is a striking and prepossessing beauty. Her looks are characterized by doe-like eyes, celestial nose, a modest sensuality about the lips, and the long reddish-golden hair associated with Pre-Raphaelite models since Rossetti's early paintings of Elizabeth

Siddal. Peter Trippi writes that, "given their three decade relationship," she "surely functioned as the artist's muse." We see her age over time from a young seductress in the earliest works to a woman of dignity and adult beauty in later paintings such as *The Soul of the Rose, or My Sweet Rose* (1908) and *The Annunciation* (1914). That Waterhouse changed his themes and approach to suit his model, rather than the other way around, is a testament to her profound influence on his work.

Head study of Miss Muriel Foster for Lamia
by John William Waterhouse, 1905.

The mystery of the model's identity was at last solved. In 1988 a pencil study by Waterhouse for his 1905 painting *Lamia* was bequeathed to the Yale Center for British Art in New Haven, Connecticut. It depicts the upturned face of the model. Her name is inscribed by Waterhouse on the paper: Miss Muriel Foster of Buxton Road, Chingford.

We are fortunate to know her name, not as a mere piece of trivia. Waterhouse's best work had for its foundation one of the most successful partnerships between artist and model in the history of painting. Muriel Foster's contribution to that partnership comes through to us today. As Rossetti wrote in another context, "Beauty like hers is genius."

LETTERS

6
Young England

The minor nineteenth-century poet and political figure Lord John Manners has long seemed to me worthy of reappraisal. That he was a minor poet was a matter of his own inclination. He published two significant volumes as a young man, *England's Trust and Other Poems*, in 1841, and *English Ballads and Other Poems*, in 1850. But although he lived until 1906 he never returned to verse. That he was, in the end, a minor political figure is a loss for Britain.

Manners was a principle member of the conservative Young England group, which he co-founded with George Smythe (later Viscount Strangford) and Alexander Baillie-Cochrane (later Baron Lamington). At Cambridge together in the 1830s, they rebelled against Utilitarianism and the new priorities of the Industrial Revolution.

By the mid-nineteenth century industrialization had drastically changed the social order, economy, and landscape of Britain. The nation's wealth had shifted from the countryside to the cities, taking with it vast populations. The sweet rural economy of manor, cottage, and craft was being undermined by policies that favored heavy industry. A decentralized society based on inherited rights and traditions, in harmony with nature, and built to the human scale was becoming increasingly centralized, mechanized, democratized, and dehumanized.

A generation earlier, Edmund Burke had written that civilization is a partnership between the dead, the living, and the yet unborn. Traditionalists of the nineteenth century viewed the progressive project as an unraveling of that partnership. The delicate system of organic institutions and relationships that underpinned the old order could not be swept away without taking with it the civilization it had brought into being. By the time Queen Victoria came to the throne in 1837 a number of political figures, artists, philosophers, and theologians were contemplating how traditional society might be recovered. Largely independent of one another they found inspiration in the aesthetics of the Middle Ages.

Young England advocated a romantic revival of feudalism and agrarianism. Manners and his friends fought to restore power to the monarchy, the peerage, and the Church of England. They promoted the interests of the countryside, its rustic economy, landed gentry, and working classes. They opposed the consolidation of power by a bourgeois oligarchy which had brought with it Blake's "dark satanic mills," slum-cities, and class warfare.

The contemporary historian Edward Barrington de Fonblanque painted a charming prose-picture of the type of society that the Young Englanders wished to create:

> The nobles of England were once more to occupy their legitimate place around the throne and in the order of chivalry; the Church was to become the revered guardian and benevolent educator of the masses; commerce and industry, literature and art, were to be fostered by generous patronage; and a grateful and contented peasantry, clustering for shelter under the shadow of lordly mansions, were to vary the monotony of their toilful lives by merry dances on the village green, and perennial feasts of roast oxen and barrels of ale provided by their munificent lords and masters, the hereditary owners of the soil.

In 1841, Manners published *England's Trust and Other Poems*, dedicated to Smythe. In his book *Young England*, to date the only book-length history of the movement, Richard Faber described the titular poem as "the most complete manifesto of Young England's basic philosophy" at that point. Manners recalled to mind "a nobler age":

> When men of stalwart hearts and steadfast faith
> Shrunk from dishonour, rather than from death,
> When to great minds obedience did not seem
> A slave's condition, or a bigot's dream...
> When kings were taught to feel the dreadful weight
> Of power derived from One than kings more great,
> And learned with reverence to wield the rod
> They dreamed entrusted to their hand by God.
>
> Each knew his place—king, peasant, peer or priest,
> The greatest owned connexion with the least;
> From rank to rank the generous feeling ran,
> And linked society as man to man.
>
> Must we then hearken to the furious cry
> Of those who clamour for 'equality?'
> Have not the people learnt how vain the trust
> On props like that which crumble into dust?
>
> Are the gradations that have marked our race,
> Since God first stamped His likeness on its face,
> Gradations hallowed by a thousand ties
> Of faith and love, and holiest sympathies,
> Seen in the Patriarch's rule, the Judge's sway
> When God himself was Israel's present stay,
> Now in the world's dotage to be cast
> As week pretences to the howling blast?
>
> No! by the names inscribed in History's page,
> Names that shall live for yet unnumbered years
> Shrined in our hearts with Crécy and Poitiers,
> Let wealth and commerce, laws and learning die
> But leave us still our old Nobility!

When Manners wrote, "leave us still our old Nobility" he did not, of course, mean that his own class alone should endure: he meant the whole system of hierarchy and heredity and mutual loyalty that ensured a place for every man and protected the ancestral rights of the dynastic farmer or craftsman just as much as the rights of the dynastic lord. The politics of "equality" not only disenfranchised the nobility but destroyed the protections that the working classes had inherited over generations.

By 1843, Manners, Smythe, and Baillie-Cochrane were all seated in Parliament. They represented a High Tory bloc within the larger Conservative party of which they were members. In a speech to the House of Commons on May 18, 1843, Manners staked out his position, extolling those "principles which, while they would render the Church triumphant, and monarchy powerful, would also restore contentment to a struggling, overworked and deluded people." A contemporary summary, in Hansard's *Parliamentary Debates*, records the substance of the speech. He argued that,

> As power was taken away from the mitre and the crown and transferred either to the people in that House or out of it, their physical and moral happiness had been lessened...He would extend the feeling of responsibility between the rich and the poor, and shorten the interval which in his opinion was growing too wide between those for whom wealth was made and those who made it.

Manners campaigned against the Mortmain Act of 1736 which put restrictions on the devising of property to charitable uses. He proposed lifting the law to encourage the establishment of religious houses. He argued that "it is inexpedient, in the present condition of the country, to continue the existing restrictions on the exercise of private charity and munificence." Manners hoped that by overturning the Act the government could not only facilitate but encourage the founding of charitable religious institutions. "In an age confessedly devoted to money-making," he said in a speech to Parliament, "I ask you to have the courage to believe in the nobler impulses of our nature; to appeal to the glorious spirit which built our cathedrals, our colleges, our convents." Although he was unsuccessful in this initial campaign, the law was eventually superseded in 1888, in part through his advocacy.

Like Charles Dickens had, in his pamphlet, *Sunday Under Three Heads*, Manners also argued that the working classes needed more leisure time. If civil society was to be nurtured it would require those conditions of leisure, festival, and camaraderie which were the natural expressions of a healthy community. In his 1843 pamphlet, *A Plea for National Holy-Days*, Manners asked: "Will the old parish church send out of its time-honoured portals and old men and women, the lads and lasses, to the merry green, where youth shall disport itself, and old age, well pleased, look on? Alas! no. Utilitarian selfishness has well nigh banished all such unproductive amusements from the land."

In Parliament, Young England attracted the attention of the MP from Shrewsbury, Benjamin Disraeli, who saw its members as potential allies. Disraeli's own philosophy of "one-nation conservatism," which he represented in the novels *Sybil* and *Coningsby*, grew out of his intellectual relationship with them. It was Disraeli who marshaled the circle into a larger political faction. As the most experienced politician among them he became the de facto leader of the group.

They also attracted the attention of critics. *The Morning Herald* wrote of Manners and Smythe: "These two gentlemen are the prime movers of *Young England*; and that tomfoolery is the political offshoot of Tractarianism. Mental dandyism is its chiefest characteristic." Tractarianism refers to the Oxford Movement in the Church of England. The Tractarians emphasized the broadly catholic inheritance of the Anglican tradition. At its best the movement inspired a revival of piety and ritual in the Church of England. Its apologists demonstrated that Anglicanism had unbroken continuity with Ancient Christianity, no less than the ultramontane Roman Catholic Church, which was, for all intents and purposes, created at the Council of Trent. (The Anglican *Book of Common Prayer* predates the *Roman Missal* by two decades). At its worst the movement displaced an authentic High Church Protestantism with the trappings of nineteenth-century Roman Catholicism; in this it may have done more harm than good.

The members of Young England were all High Anglicans of one school or another. Manners and Smythe belonged to the Oxford Movement. Manners imagined the church engendering new quasi-monastic orders and institutions that would transform industrial cities, providing charitable services and cultural roots to increasingly atomized populations.

Clearly the Young Englanders were romantics. In later years, Baillie-Cochrane wrote that they had desired to lighten the servitude and add to the enjoyments of the people: "in fact, to restore 'Merrie England.'" They did not accomplish anything so grand. The word "dream" appears often in assessments of the group. De Fonblanque described Young England as "a pretty and harmless dream." They were not without realism or political skill, however.

During their Parliamentary careers the Young Englanders were engaged in the day-to-day business of government. They had successes and failures. The Factory Act of 1847 which limited the working hours of women and children was passed after years of advocacy by the group.

Young England was not opposed to industrial capitalism per se. Disraeli wanted to unite the "aristocracy of wealth" with the aristocracy of birth and instill in the former the sense of paternalism and *noblesse oblige* for the working classes that the latter possessed. Manners also wanted the great capitalists to take on a neo-feudal responsibility for their workers. He was impressed by the Grant brothers of Manchester, affluent merchants on whom Dickens had based the magnanimous Cheeryble brothers in *Nicholas Nickleby*. But Manners doubted that the marketplace could ever produce the stability necessary for the emergence of an actual "aristocracy of wealth." He wrote to his brother Granby, after a tour of Manchester cotton mills in 1841, "the worst of this manufacturing feudalism is its uncertainty, and the moment a cotton lord is down, there's an end to his dependents' very subsistence: in legislating, this great difference between an agricultural and a trading aristocracy ought not to be lost sight of." In the 1840s the working population was divided roughly evenly between the traditional economy of the countryside and the new economy of the factory town. The Young Englanders were adamant that this balance not tip too far toward the city. Without the equilibrium of the unchanging rural economy they believed that the protean upheavals of the factory system would lead to social unrest. To this end, Baillie-Cochrane said, "The only way to arrest the march of revolution in this country was to decide at once against all concession...if the agricultural party were only true to themselves, no influence... would be able to destroy them." Even long after the heyday of Young England, Manners was confident that with proper leadership the "agricultural classes" could "fight for the existing order" against "democratic Revolution."

In truth the Factory Act was a rearguard action by the agricultural party. By 1847 laws were in place that would cripple the rural economy and put the industrial party firmly in control of Britain's destiny. The first of these was the Reform Act of 1832 which had stripped parliamentary representation from small rural boroughs and doubled the representation of many industrial cities. The second was the abolition of the Corn Laws in 1846; free traders finally achieved their long-held ambition to remove tariffs on foreign grain, tilting the market to the disadvantage of British farmers.

Young England was dormant by the end of the 1840s. Disraeli went on to political glory, becoming prime minister in 1868, and again in 1874, but by that time he had left Young England behind. Manners had a long, useful, and distinguished career in government under several Conservative administrations. He served as First Commissioner of Works under Lord Derby and Postmaster-General under Disraeli and Lord Salisbury. Disraeli offered him the viceroyalty of India but he declined. His last public office was Chancellor of the Duchy of Lancaster under Lord Salisbury. In 1891, Queen Victoria knighted him to the Order of the Garter. By that point he had inherited his father's peerage, becoming the seventh Duke of Rutland. Despite prominent careers, however, neither Manners, Smythe, nor Baillie-Cochrane ever controlled policy to the extent that they could advance the agenda of Young England.

7

A Ghost Story for Christmas

Every December we find ourselves in thrall to Charles Dickens and his seasonal classic, *A Christmas Carol*. Whether you read the novel every year or encounter it in one of its many adaptations and pastiches for stage or screen, there is no avoiding it. It is one of those rare stories that everyone knows, whether they have read the book or not: the miser Scrooge is visited on Christmas Eve by ghosts and apparitions who show him visions of his own past, present, and future, and those of the people with whom his life is intertwined, rekindling in his heart the warmth of Christian charity.

Dickens was a great keeper of Christmas. Among his earliest writings, the newspaper columns collected in 1836 as *Sketches By Boz*, there is a commemoration of the holiday which contains many of the themes he would later revisit in *A Christmas Carol*. He writes, "Christmas time! That man must be a misanthrope indeed, in whose breast something like a jovial feeling is not roused—in whose mind some pleasant associations are not awakened—by the recurrence of Christmas...Petty jealousies and discords are forgotten; social feelings are awakened, in bosoms to which they have long been strangers."

In the first half of the nineteenth-century, Christmas was not universally or extravagantly celebrated in England. Of course midwinter had been a time of revelry in northern Europe since pagan antiquity, marking the beginning of the return of the sun, and the retreat of darkness. But Christmas was never as significant as Easter in the Christian liturgical year. And while a history of merrymaking endured, especially in the countryside, where the rhythms of nature were better felt, in the busy commercial hub of London it was for many people just another day of work.

By the time Dickens wrote *A Christmas Carol* in 1843 there were signs of a revival of the holiday in the popular culture. Queen Victoria and her husband Prince Albert introduced the Christmas Tree to England from Germany in 1840. Two decades earlier, American author Washington Irving had recorded the surviving traditions of Christmas in rural England during his long residence in the country. "Old Christmas" was published in 1819 in Irving's *Sketch Book of Geoffrey Crayon*, which also contained "The Legend of Sleepy Hollow" and "Rip Van Winkle."

Dickens himself included a marvelous description of Christmas festivities in his first novel, *The Posthumous Papers of the Pickwick Club*, or, *The Pickwick Papers*, published in 1837. This great sprawling comic novel follows Samuel Pickwick, retired businessman and philanthropist, who, together with members of his eponymous London club, sets out on a series of misadventures to enlarge "his sphere of observation, to the advancement of knowledge and the diffusion of learning." In one episode Pickwick spends Christmas at the manor of the rough, generous country squire Mr Wardle. Here family, friends, tenants, and servants gather together as one social body, undisrupted by the class warfare of the industrial revolution, under the benevolent lordship of Wardle. There is dancing, kissing under the mistletoe, a raucous game of blind man's buff, quaffing of wassail, feasting, and storytelling.

It is interesting that both Dickens and Irving relegated Christmas festivities to the countryside, where the holiday and the great old manor houses in which it was still kept, were depicted as survivals of a bygone age. In the early nineteenth century this was probably accurate enough.

A Christmas Carol changed the way Christmas was celebrated in England. Dickens had intended it to do as much. He did not merely want to glorify the folk traditions of the season. The immediate impetus for the novel was his sympathy and concern for the poor, in particular children. It was a passion nearer to his own heart than anyone could have guessed at the time.

Dickens was born in Portsmouth in 1812 during a period of maritime build-up at the end of the Napoleonic Wars. His good-natured but improvident father, John Dickens, kept the family in middle-class comfort with a well paid job at the Navy Pay Office. For the first ten years of his life Charles Dickens thrived in an atmosphere of love and encouragement. He romped in nature. He read voraciously: *The Arabian Nights*, *Robinson Crusoe*, Henry Fielding. He wrote stories and staged drawing room theatricals. But John Dickens found himself increasingly in debt. He moved the family to London in 1822 where they struggled to make ends meet. In 1824 he was prosecuted by his creditors and sent to the Marshalsea debtors prison. The entire family lived with him at the Marshalsea except for twelve-year old Charles who was put to work. A job was found for him at Warren's Blacking Warehouse, near the present-day Embankment tube station. He was paid six shillings per week to work ten hour days glueing labels to cans of boot polish in appalling conditions. He never spoke of the experience but he gave an account of it to his friend and biographer John Forster:

> The blacking-warehouse was the last house on the left-hand side of the way, at old Hungerford Stairs. It was a crazy, tumble-down old house, abutting of course on the river, and literally overrun with rats. Its wainscoted rooms, and its rotten floors and staircase, and the old grey rats swarming down in the cellars, and the sound of their squeaking and scuffling coming up the stairs at all times, and the dirt and decay of the place, rise up visibly before me, as if I were there again.

In time, John Dickens paid off his creditors and was released from the Marshalsea. Charles was allowed to leave the blacking warehouse and return to a semblance of a normal childhood. But the experience changed him forever. Feelings of abandonment and betrayal and loneliness and fear haunted him long after.

The success of Dickens's early novels made him a very

rich man. He relished the role of a celebrity and a gentleman and spent lavishly on himself and his family. But the wretched children whose lives he had briefly and traumatically shared were never far from his mind. He always considered it his duty to employ both pen and purse toward a remedy for the ills of society.

When he wrote *A Christmas Carol*, he became, in the words of the actor and author Simon Callow,

> a spokesman, not just for the oppressed and the disadvantaged, but for the essential integrity of a nation in the throes of radical transformation. There was a widespread unease at the way in which capitalism was evolving, at the loss of community and the inter-relatedness of the groups within it. The writing of the book sprang directly from his horror at the condition of children in the mines. Christmas, Dickens insisted, was mocked unless the absolute dregs of society were rehabilitated and the root causes of their rejection and elimination by society addressed.

This was something that Dickens believed could only be accomplished by the changing of hearts—and a changing of the way that business was done. He was no proto-Marxist. Callow notes, "Dickens didn't believe you could fob off your personal responsibilities on to the state. He...didn't believe in a welfare state, but in absolute direct human action." How different money is in the hands of Scrooge than it is in those of Mr Pickwick, or Scrooge's first employer, the magnanimous old Fezziwig.

It is no coincidence that Dickens's greatest call to charity was in a book that also called readers to feast and festivity. All of these are expressions of an expansiveness, an overabundance, a pouring forth, of the heart. One cannot exist without the other.

The monstrousness of Scrooge, as we find him at the beginning of *A Christmas Carol*, is in his stinginess of heart as well as money. Likewise, his reformation at the end of the novel is a conversion of the heart. Charity and benevolence and festivity and love and joy pour forth in equal measure. He becomes the Dickensian ideal: a "whole" man.

"Christmas Eve at Mr Wardle's"
(Illustration for The Pickwick Papers) by Phiz, 1837.

It was a stroke of genius on the author's part to bring about this transformation with the aid of the supernatural. There is an atavistic power to the evocation of ghosts at this time of year, much as there is to the reenactment of the ancient feast.

I have always liked the English custom of telling ghost stories on Christmas Eve. It is not as popular as it used to be. We think of it as a Victorian custom, largely because of *A Christmas*

Carol, but it is much, much older. Like other folkways it has receded from the forefront of the culture but we still encounter it.

Over the years, the BBC has adapted a number of the ghost stories of M.R. James for television. These adaptations culminated in a very fine series in 2000 featuring Sir Christopher Lee, titled *Ghost Stories for Christmas*. James had written his stories as seasonal entertainments during a long tenure as don and provost at King's College, Cambridge. The BBC recreated James's original readings for the series: a group of scholars gather in his book-lined rooms at King's, which are decorated for Christmas, lit by candles, and a blazing fire in the hearth; they pour glasses of port, make themselves comfortable, and listen while James, played by Sir Christopher, tells a story. There are no special effects. In fact, there is very little to the production except for an intimate atmosphere; James's words; a haunting and sublime arrangement of the Lyke-Wake Dirge, by the Anglican choral-composer Geoffrey Burgon, as theme music; and Sir Christopher's inimitable baritone voice. The result is one of my three or four favorite series ever to air on television (the others being *Sherlock Holmes* starring Jeremy Brett and *Poirot* starring David Suchet, of course).

The telling of ghost stories has a corollary in other customs that cast an eerie mood over the Christmas vigil. The parlor game snap-dragon was mentioned by Shakespeare and Dryden, and has an entry in Dr Johnson's dictionary. It was already a well known game in the nineteenth century when Dickens wrote of it in *The Pickwick Papers*. Snap-dragon is played with a bowl of raisins, soaked in brandy. The lights are dimmed and the brandy is set on fire, producing an uncanny blue flame. Participants attempt to snatch raisins out of the fire and extinguish them by popping them into their mouths and eating them. Writing in his journal, *The Tatler*, in the eighteenth century, Sir Richard Steele explained, "the wantonness of the thing was to see each other look like a demon, as we burnt ourselves, and snatched out the fruit."

In *Pickwick Papers* Dickens connected the playing of snap-dragon and the telling of "old stories" in his depiction of a Christmas Eve revel at Dingley Dell Farm, the Kentish manor house of Mr Wardle. After the dance, when the mood of the assembled guests had settled, Dickens writes:

> [T]here was a great game at snap-dragon, and when fingers enough were burned with that, and all the raisins were gone, they sat down by the huge fire of blazing logs to a substantial supper, and a mighty bowl of wassail, something smaller than an ordinary wash-house copper, in which the hot apples were hissing and bubbling with a rich look, and a jolly sound, that were perfectly irresistible.
>
> "This," said Mr Pickwick, looking round him, "this is, indeed, comfort."
>
> "Our invariable custom," replied Mr Wardle. "Everybody sits down with us on Christmas Eve, as you see them now—servants and all; and here we wait, until the clock strikes twelve, to usher Christmas in, and beguile the time with forfeits and old stories. Trundle, my boy, rake up the fire."

I think these traditions serve a ritual purpose similar to the antimasque in a masque. They are part of a performance, a folk ceremony, outside the formal liturgy of the church, that commemorates the triumph of divine order over the fallen world.

The masque was a form of entertainment popular in Tudor and Jacobean England. It was partly theater and partly dance. It would begin with an antimasque: a short vignette that represented the world in chaos. This might involve portrayals of drunken disorder, witchcraft, or war. The masque proper would then begin with the arrival of the king and queen and courtiers, disguised as ancient gods. They would conquer the antimasque and bring order to the symbolic universe of the hall—a transformation represented by a formal dance.

In the Christian liturgical year, the season of Advent that leads up to Christmas, is a time of vigilance and preparation. It is a solemn season. We are given the opportunity to reflect on the hope and hardship of those who lived in the world before Christ was born into it: a world of darkness, confusion, and chaos. Every year we reenact the vigil of those who waited faithfully for the Savior through dark days. When Christmas Eve gives way to Christmas, and we remember the arrival of God in the world, darkness gives way to light, solemnity to celebration, fast to feasting, ghost stories to carols, chaos to Godly order.

8
Dickens and the Stage

Charles Dickens always wanted to be an actor. As a teenager in the late 1820s he was working in London as a lawyer's clerk and a courtroom stenographer. In his free time he attended the theater with fanatic devotion. Dickens later wrote that he "went to some theatre every night...for at least three years." Actors like William Macready, Charles Kean, Thomas Cooke, and Charles Mathews dominated the stage of this period. Dickens was particularly fond of Mathews, a veteran actor famous for his "monopolylogues," one man shows in which he played all of the characters. Dickens would go wherever "there was the best acting; and always to see Mathews, whenever he played." The monopolylogue was a form that naturally appealed to Dickens, who would entertain his coworkers by mimicking various London types, and who, later, as a prolific novelist, would recite his dialogue out loud, in character, as he wrote it.

By 1831 Dickens had begun to think of a career as an actor "in quite a business-like way." That year he wrote to George Bartley, manager of the Covent Garden Theatre, to ask for an audition. Dickens told Bartley that he possessed "a strong perception of character and oddity, and a natural power of reproducing in my own person what I observed in others." Bartley agreed to see him. When the day of the audition came, however, Dickens was sick with a cold. He rescheduled for the following season. By then the moment had passed. In the interim he was hired as a reporter for his uncle's newspaper, *The Mirror of Parliament*. So Dickens went on to become the most celebrated writer of his age, instead of the most celebrated actor. And yet, he was never fully rid of his early ambition.

Beginning with his first novel, that magnificent, hilarious, deeply human portrait of English life, *The Pickwick Papers*, almost all of Dickens's novels were adapted for the stage. Often they were produced immediately upon publication, sometimes before the serialized chapters had finished running in the magazines that published them, and as often as not without the author's permission. Within weeks of the publication of *A Christmas Carol*, eight different adaptations were on stage in London. Dickens at least had authorized one of them.

These stage productions were invariably successful at the box office, so hungry was the public for the author's work. The theater of his day must have been a perfect mirror for Dickens's stories. He had drawn so much of his style of writing—the larger-than-life characters, the layering of dark melodrama and light comedy (what he called "streaky bacon"), the phantasmagoric set-pieces—from the theater. Simon Callow, in his superb biography, *Charles Dickens and the Great Theatre of the World*, writes that, "Every episode of *Pickwick* introduced new editions of old stage characters; the spirit of Charles Mathews was everywhere in its pages."

At the beginning of his career as a novelist Dickens also wrote for the stage. While he was writing *The Pickwick Papers* he composed the libretto for *The Village Coquettes*, an operetta by John Hullah, that was staged in 1836. The following year, while he was writing *Oliver Twist*, he wrote a farce for the St James Theatre called *Is She His Wife?* Callow believes that Dickens was too stage-struck, too reverent of the theater to make it his own: the plays "suffered from his abject adoration of the theatre of his day, which he dutifully reproduced. It would be hard to find a sentence in any essay, novel, story or letter of Dickens's that does not have some authentic flavour, but you will search the plays in vain for a single Dickensian turn of phrase."

By 1838 Dickens had largely sublimated his theatrical imagination into his novels. That year he was writing *Oliver Twist* and *Nicholas Nickleby* simultaneously, releasing monthly installments of each. For the next twenty years he kept to this pace, publishing as many as three books per year. But he continued to seek out any small opportunities he could find to be involved with the theater.

In 1845 Dickens and a group of literary and artistic friends staged a production of Ben Johnson's play, *Every Man in his Humour*, for charity. Dickens took on the role of the great blustering braggart, Captain Bobadil. Performances were held in Soho and West End theaters. At one performance Queen Victoria was in attendance. Dickens went on to play Sir Epicure Mammon in Johnson's *The Alchemist* and Justice Shallow in William Shakespeare's *Merry Wives of Windsor* for similar charity productions. In 1856 he collaborated with Wilkie Collins on an amateur production of Collins's new play, *The Frozen Deep*. The word amateur is used only in the strict sense that no money was recouped. The play was staged at Tavistock House, Dickens's home in the Bloomsbury neighborhood of London. In order to accommodate a thirty-foot stage and seating for around a hundred people, Dickens spared no expense to renovate the house. Sets were created by Clarkson Stansfield, who, Callow writes, "as well as being the most distinguished marine painter of his time and an RA, had earlier been the chief scene-painter at Drury Lane. Costumes came from Nathan's, the premier theatrical costumiers, new gas-lines (to the disapproval of the fire office-surveyor) were laid down, machinery and props were loaned from the Theatre Royal Haymarket."

The impetus behind Wilkie Collins's script for *The Frozen Deep* was a controversy that had recently arisen over the doomed Franklin Expedition of the previous decade. Captain Sir John Franklin and a team of 128 men had set out in 1845 to chart the Northwest Passage through the Arctic Sea. Their ships became icebound in the Victoria Straight and all men were lost. In the early 1850s the first discoveries of their fate were made by search parties. A report to the Admiralty that was made public in 1854 suggested that the stranded party had resorted to cannibalism. Lady Franklin protested vigorously against this calumny on her husband's memory. Like many members of the public, Dickens was incensed at the report, and devoted many words to defending Captain Franklin and his crew. *The Frozen Deep* portrayed the noble character of British men in a similar situation. Dickens would play the tragic hero, an explorer stranded in the arctic, who sacrifices himself to save another man, his rival for the love of a woman no less.

The first performances were played to audiences of friends, including members of Parliament and government ministers, in January of 1857. This was followed in July by a command performance for Queen Victoria and Prince Albert, their family, and guests, including King Leopold of Belgium and Prince Frederick William of Prussia. In July and August six public performances were staged, at the Royal Gallery of Illustration in London, and Free Trade Hall in Manchester, for paying audiences, to benefit the widow of Dickens's friend, playwright Douglas Jerrold.

By all contemporary accounts Dickens's performance was excellent. A reviewer for *The Leader* wrote that what he accomplished "might open a new era for the stage, if the stage had the wisdom to profit by it." There was not a dry eye in the house by the end. "[I]t was a good thing," Dickens wrote, "to have a couple of thousand people...in the palm of one's hand." Twenty-five years after missing an audition at the Covent Garden Theatre, Dickens had finally tread the boards, and proven himself as an actor. When the engagements were over, he felt "shipwrecked."

Shortly afterward Dickens gave a series of public readings from his own work, to benefit Great Ormond Street Hospital, which proved very successful. He began to see in the medium of staged readings a natural outlet for his theatrical ambitions. He planned what would be an ongoing and lucrative speaking tour. For ten months between April of 1858 and February of 1859, he held 129 readings across the United Kingdom.

"Readings" is not really a sufficient word for what Dickens did at these appearances. He transformed himself into his characters—into David Copperfield, into Scrooge from *A Christmas Carol*, Fagin from *Oliver Twist*, and countless others. Charles Kent, who was in the audience, wrote:

> Fagin, the Jew, was there completely, audibly, visibly before us, by a sort of transformation... Whenever [Dickens] spoke [as the character], there started before us high-shouldered with contracted chest, with birdlike claws, eagerly anticipating by their every movement the passionate words fiercely struggling for

utterance at his lips—that most villainous old tutor of young thieves, receiver of stolen goods, and very devil incarnate: his features distorted with rage, his penthouse eyebrows (those wonderful eyebrows!) working like the antennae of some deadly reptile, his whole aspect, half-vulpine, half-vulture-like, in its hungry wickedness.

Charles Dickens at the podium he designed for his speaking tours.

Standing alone on the stage, behind an unobtrusive desk that he had designed himself, Dickens shifted mercurially between characters as he conjured stories for the audience.

Simon Callow quotes Thomas Carlyle telling Dickens, "you carry a whole company under your hat." The effect could be frightening or funny or both. A reviewer for *The Times* called it a "return to the practice of Bardic times." A more immediate association might have been to the theater of Charles Mathews—these were monopolylogues.

Throughout the last decade of his life, despite increasingly poor health, Dickens continued to mount major speaking tours. He visited America in 1868, giving 76 readings in New York, Boston, and other cities, then returned to launch a final tour in Britain. In the 1860s, he added a sensational and horrifying segment to his stage repertoire: the murder of Nancy by Bill Sikes from *Oliver Twist*. Charles Kent left a record of the performance:

> As for the Author's embodiment of Sikes—
> the burly ruffian with thews of iron and voice
> of Stentor—it was only necessary to hear
> that infuriated voice, and watch the appalling
> blows dealt by his imaginary bludgeon in the
> perpetration of the crime, to realise the force,
> the power, the passion, informing the creative
> mind of the Novelist at once in the original
> conception of the character, and then, so many
> years afterwards, in its equally astonishing
> representation.
>
> It was in the portrayal of Nancy, however,
> that the genius of the Author-Actor found the
> opportunity, beyond all others, for its most signal
> manifestation. Only that the catastrophe was in
> itself, by necessity so utterly revolting, there
> would have been something exquisitely pathetic
> in many parts of that affecting delineation. The
> character was revealed with perfect consistency
> throughout—from the scene of suppressed
> emotion upon the steps of London Bridge, when
> she is scared with the eltrich horror of her
> forebodings, down to her last gasping, shrieking
> apostrophes, to "Bill, dear Bill," when she sinks,
> blinded by blood, under the murderous blows

dealt upon her upturned face by her brutal paramour.

Then, again, the horror experienced by the assassin afterwards! So far as it went, it was as grand a reprehension of all murderers as hand could well have penned or tongue have uttered. It had about it something of the articulation of an avenging voice not against Sikes only, but against all who ever outraged, or ever dreamt of outraging, the sanctity of human life. And it was precisely this which tended to sublimate an incident otherwise of the ghastliest horror into a homily of burning eloquence, the recollection of which among those who once saw it revealed through the lips, the eyes, the whole aspect of Charles Dickens will not easily be obliterated.

These nightly displays took an immense toll on the author. He was already suffering health problems. By the time of the farewell tour he had to lie down for half an hour after every performance to bring his pulse back to normal. There was swelling in his extremities. He slurred words and had difficulty reading. Nevertheless he pressed on and by some miracle or force of will his stage presence did not seem to suffer at all.

Dickens gave his final reading on March 15, 1870, at St James's Hall in London. He performed *A Christmas Carol* and the trial scene from *The Pickwick Papers*. When it was over he addressed a few closing remarks to the audience. His speech ostensibly marked the end of his performing career and the resumption of his writing. But as Callow notes, "it was a sort of swansong, and everyone knew it." Dickens said:

> Ladies and gentlemen—It would be worse than idle—for it would be hypocritical and unfeeling— if I were to disguise that I close this episode in my life with feelings of very considerable pain. For some fifteen years, in this hall and in many kindred places, I have had the honour of presenting my own cherished ideas before you

for your recognition, and, in closely observing your reception of them, have enjoyed an amount of artistic delight and instruction which, perhaps, is given to few men to know. In this task, and in every other I have ever undertaken, as a faithful servant of the public, always imbued with a sense of duty to them, and always striving to do his best, I have been uniformly cheered by the readiest response, the most generous sympathy, and the most stimulating support. Nevertheless, I have thought it well, at the full flood-tide of your favour, to retire upon those older associations between us, which date from much further back than these, and henceforth to devote myself exclusively to the art that first brought us together. Ladies and gentlemen, in but two short weeks from this time I hope that you may enter, in your own homes, on a new series of readings, at which my assistance will be indispensable; but from these garish lights I vanish now for evermore, with a heartfelt, grateful, respectful, and affectionate farewell.

Dickens died of a stroke at his home in Kent less than three months later, leaving his final novel, *The Mystery of Edwin Drood*, unfinished.

9
An Account of Ye Olde Cheshire Cheese

Down a narrow little alley in London called Wine Office Court, entered through Fleet Street, is a venerable and time-worn pub called Ye Olde Cheshire Cheese. It is my favorite establishment in the Square Mile, a sentiment I know is widely shared. The Cheese is steeped in history, dating back at least to the reign of King Charles II. (It was built on the ashes of an earlier pub shortly after the Great Fire of 1666.) Often I have enjoyed a quiet lunch here in the atmospheric front rooms or a drink in one of the barrooms after Evensong at St Paul's. The labyrinth of cellars and sub-cellars was the undercroft of a thirteenth-century monastery that once occupied the site. The pub is popular with City financial workers and attracts sightseers for a pint where Dickens and Dr Johnson drank before them. It has drawn a similar clientele for more than a century.

The Cheese has long-standing literary associations. Samuel Johnson, in the eighteenth century, and Charles Dickens, in the nineteenth, were the most famous regulars, but Oliver Goldsmith, Edmund Burke, James Boswell, William Makepeace Thackeray, Wilkie Collins, Mark Twain, Lord Tennyson, Sir Arthur Conan Doyle, W.B. Yeats, and P.G. Wodehouse all refreshed themselves here over the years.

When the journalist Cyrus Redding took up residence nearby in 1806, there were still a few old men who remembered Dr Johnson and his circle meeting at the Cheese years before. In his memoir, *Fifty Years' Recollections, Literary and Personal*, Redding wrote,

I often dined at the Cheshire Cheese. Johnson and his friends, I was informed, used to do the same, and I was told I should see individuals who had met them there. This I found to be correct. The company was more select than in later times. Johnson had been dead about twenty years, but there were Fleet Street tradesmen who well remembered both Johnson and Goldsmith in this place of entertainment.

There are mementos of that time in the tavern today. Entering the Cheese through Wine Office Court, one finds oneself in a hallway with rooms opening on either side. To the right is a cozy little barroom where a sea-coal fire burns in the hearth all year round. A notice carved above the door reads, "Gentlemen only served in this bar." Presumably it is not enforced.

To the left is the chop room. It was here that Dr Johnson was said to have held court. The room remains largely unchanged to this day. Gloomy light from the alley, candlelight from the tables, and the antique smell of the coal fire from across the hall, create a timeless atmosphere. A painting of Dr Johnson hangs over his regular seat at the far end of the communal table along the right-hand wall. The space to his left was regularly occupied by Charles Dickens a generation later. A plaque in the wall above the bench identifies Dickens's customary seat. It is a nice place to sit, in the company of these writers, separated only by time.

Dickens frequented a number of Fleet Street taverns, though he was a most modest eater and drinker. Much of his working life was spent in the neighborhood, first as a young clerk, at the inns of court, then as an editor, conducting the magazines, *Household Words* and *All the Year Round*. A scene in his 1859 novel *A Tale of Two Cities* is set at the Cheshire Cheese. Dickens writes,

> Drawing his arm through his own, he took him down Ludgate Hill to Fleet Street, and so, up a covered way, into a tavern. Here they were shown into a little room, where Charles Darnay was soon recruiting his strength with a good plain

dinner and good wine; while Carton sat opposite to him at the same table, with his separate bottle of port before him, and his fully half-insolent manner upon him.

The celebrity of Dickens was such that tourists sought out his old haunts in the decades after his death. The American artist Joseph Pennell wrote a colorful account of the Cheese for *Harper's Weekly* in 1887:

On my first coming to London, I had fortified myself, not with a course of English history, but by re-reading *Pickwick*. My first Sunday morning, about one o'clock, I found myself in Chancery Lane outside the entrance to Lincoln's Inn, in the company of the proverbial solitary policeman and convivial Ye Olde Cheshire Cheesecat. On my asking the policeman where in the world I could get something to eat—as it is well known one must starve in London on Sunday before one and after three—he gave me the inevitable answer, 'Down to the bottom, first to your left, under the lamp, up the passage, and there you are!' After he had repeated these mysterious directions two or three times, and had found me hopelessly ignorant of his meaning, he did what I have very seldom known a London policeman to do—a proof of his loneliness; he walked to the end of Chancery Lane with me, and there being no one in Fleet Street, pointed out the sign of the Cheshire Cheese. A push at the door, and I have passed into another world. I was in a narrow hall, at the far end of which was a quaint bar, where, framed in by small panes, were two very pretty, but I cannot say fascinating barmaids—I never could be fascinated by the ordinary English barmaid. Suddenly a waiter with a very short nose came out of another room and screamed up the stairs: 'Cotherum steak. Boatherum foozlum mash. Fotherum coozlum, botherum steak!' and then remarked to me: 'Lunch, sir? Yes, sir. Thank you, sir. What can I get you, sir? Steak, sir; chop, sir; kidney, sir; potatoes, sir, cooked in their jackets, sir? Yes, sir; thank you, sir.' Then up the stairs he added: 'Underdone steak one!' Then to me again: 'Walk in, sir. Take a seat, sir. Paper, sir? Lloyd's, sir? Reynolds', sir? Yes, sir.'

I had begun to look around me. I found I had stumbled on just what I had determined to make a hunt for. I was in one of the greenbaize-curtained boxes into which Mr. Pickwick was always dropping under the guidance of Sam Weller, whose 'knowledge of London was extensive and peculiar.' Unless you have a Sam Weller at your elbow you will not very easily find the Cheshire Cheese, the last of the London chop-houses, even though it is in Baedeker. In the opposite corner was, not Mr. Pickwick, but one of those respectable shabby old gentlemen you never see outside of London. The waiter asked him in the same confidential tone, 'if he would not have a half-bitter! if he would not like to see yesterday's Times? A most interestin' article in it, sir, Mr. Price, sir.' Then Mr. Price's half-bitter came in a dented old pewter pot, and along with it an exaggerated wine-glass; and Mr. Price held the pewter in the air, and a softly murmuring stream flowed from the one into the other. Beyond the box I was in I saw other hard straight-backed seats, and between them other most beautifully clean, white clothcovered tables, at all of which were three or four rather quiet and sedate, but after their manner sociable, Englishmen, everybody seeming to know everybody else in the place. Everything seemed happy, even to the cat purring on the hearth, and the brass kettle singing on the hob. Perhaps I should except the restless waiter, who, when anyone came in, rushed to the bottom of the stairs and gave his unearthly yell. Soon down the same stairs came the translation of the yell in the shape of the steak I had ordered, and with it the potatoes in their jackets, all on old blue willow-ware plates.

'Your steak, sir. Yes, sir. Anything else, sir? Napkin, sir? Oh, serviette! Yes, sir. All Americans like them, sir.'

And so I found for the first time that napkins and bread, freely bestowed in decent restaurants at home, are in England looked upon as costly luxuries.

I have returned again and again to the Cheshire Cheese, and have, moreover, tried to induce others to go there with me. For if the place is not haunted, as it is said to be, by the shades of Ben Jonson and Herrick, of Samuel Johnson and Boswell, the waiter is perfectly willing, for a consideration, to point out to you the stains of their wigs on the wall. It is certain that Dickens, Forster, Tom Hood, Wilkie Collins, and many other worthies did frequent it, while Sala periodically puffs it, and a host of other lights have written about it. In my own small way I have endeavoured to lead some modern junior novelists and poets there, to show them how near they could come to some of the great masters whom they apparently worship so thoroughly. But on the only occasion when I succeeded in placing one probably in the seat of Goldsmith or Herrick, he sniffed at the chops and remarked that if Johnson had had a napkin it would have been better for his personal appearance.

I hardly know myself what is the attraction of the place, for you can only get chops and steaks, kidneys and sausages, or on Saturdays a gigantic pudding, to eat your money's worth of which you must have the appetite of a

Gargantua, or, on Shrove Tuesdays, pancakes. If you should happen to want anything else, you would probably get the answer which Mr. Sala says was given to a friend of his who asked (at the Cock) for a hard boiled egg with his salad: 'A hegg! If Halbert Hedward 'imself wuz to cum 'ere he couldn't 'ave a hegg.' Whoever really cares to see the last of the Old London chop-houses, let him, when next in London, look up the sign of YE OLDE CHESHYRE CHEESE.

The literary history of the Cheese continued after the time of Pennell's writing. In 1890, W.B. Yeats and Ernest Rhys founded the Rhymer's Club at the Cheese. P.G. Wodehouse dined there in the early twentieth century. He remarked to a friend, in 1927, "Yesterday, I looked in at the Garrick at lunchtime, took one glance of loathing at the mob, and went off to lunch by myself at the Cheshire Cheese."

The customary seats of Dr Johnson (beneath his portrait) and Charles Dickens (marked by a book) in the Chop Room of Ye Olde Cheshire Cheese.

10
The Last
of the Coaching Inns

It is remarkable that the Tabard Inn mentioned by Chaucer in *The Canterbury Tales* was still doing business on Borough High Street in Southwark as late as 1873. It was at the Tabard, then under the proprietorship of a man named Harry Bailey, that Chaucer's pilgrims first met as they began the pilgrimage from London to Canterbury. Chaucer was writing between 1387 and 1400, at which point the Tabard, founded in 1307, was an established presence on the south bank of the Thames.

In the prologue to *The Canterbury Tales*, Chaucer writes:

> Befell that in that season, on a day,
> In Southwark at the Tabard as I lay
> Ready to wenden on my pilgrimage
> To Canterbury with full devout courage,
> At night was come into that hostelery
> Well nine-and-twenty in a company
> Of sundry folk, by adventure fallen
> Into fellowship, and pilgrims were they all,
> That toward Canterbury would ride.

The Medieval structure was destroyed in the fire that razed much of Medieval Southwark in 1676, ten years after the Great Fire of London. It was immediately rebuilt on the same foundations. We do not know how much salvaged materials from the original structure were incorporated into the second. Presumably some.

As Chaucer's verse suggests Southwark was a point of entry into the City of London where journeys would begin and end. Many similar inns catered to travelers there. Next door to the Tabard was the George where it is said that Shakespeare drank and dined while he lived in the Borough. In fact the inn yards, often surrounded on three sides by the galleried façade of an inn, served as theaters in the Elizabethan period.

The rebuilt Tabard Inn and its neighbors would have enjoyed a brisk business as stagecoach lines were established in the seventeenth century. The word stagecoach refers to the "stages" by which the route was divided. A coach, normally pulled by four horses, would travel from one station to another, change horses, allow the passengers to rest, then continue to the next station. In this way a coach could maintain an average speed of about five miles per hour, traveling sixty or seventy miles in a day.

At each station would be a coaching inn. An innkeeper with capital, or a family of innkeepers, might run coaches between establishments in multiple cities. The American author James Fenimore Cooper traveled between four different inns kept by members of the Wright family on a coach journey between Canterbury and London in 1828. At coaching inns travelers found comfort and refreshment. Cooper praised the simple pleasures of tea "served redolent of home and former days. The hissing urn, the delicious toast, the fragrant beverage, the warm sea-coal fire, and the perfect snugness of everything, were indeed grateful."

In the late eighteenth century mail coaches began to carry postal deliveries throughout Britain. This was brought about by the instigation of John Palmer, a theater impresario from Bath, who suggested and successfully demonstrated the idea to the Post Office in the early 1780s. Prior to that date mail was carried by relay riders on horseback. By coach the distances could be traversed in half the time. By 1785 there was service from London to Norwich, Liverpool, Leeds, Dover, Portsmouth, Poole, Exeter, Gloucester, Worcester, Holyhead, and Carlisle.

Mail coaches carried passengers, but unlike regular passenger coaches they were not operated for the comfort of travelers, but for the swift delivery of the mail. This meant they traveled much faster. The experience of riding on a mail coach could be exhilarating or harrowing. That experience inspired one of the great literary essays of the nineteenth century, "The English Mail-Coach," by Thomas De Quincey.

Robin Jarvis wrote an excellent account of the piece and its composition for *The Public Domain Review*:

> In the last quarter of 1849 Thomas De Quincey published two separate essays in *Blackwood's Edinburgh Magazine*, a leading Tory periodical. These two essays, entitled "The English Mail-Coach, or the Glory of Motion" and "The Vision of Sudden Death," were revised and amalgamated five years later to produce one of the author's most memorable and idiosyncratic pieces. "The English Mail-Coach" is at once a celebration of that form of transport and an elegy for its demise, since by the time De Quincey published his essay the railways had already spread across the country and shunted the mail-coach into the sidings of history...
>
> "The English Mail-Coach" is in four parts. In the first, De Quincey explains his fascination with mail-coaches and recalls his delight in using them—insisting always, against the grain of class preference, on an outside seat—to go to and from Oxford in his student days. He relates his obsession to the pleasures of unprecedented speed, with the thrill of "possible though indefinite danger"; the visual stimulation of "grand effects," as deserted roads at night are momentarily lit up by coach-lamps; the sheer spectacle of "animal beauty and power"; the sense of participating in a great national system, akin to a living organism; and the additional excitement of bringing news, good or bad, from the battlefront (during the Napoleonic Wars) to local communities far and wide.
>
> In the second section of the essay, "Going Down with Victory," De Quincey elaborates on

the adrenalin-fuelled experience of bearing tidings of war, kindling joy all along the route "like fire racing along a train of gunpowder," and describes the more ambivalent experience of giving one woman a partial account of the "imperfect victory" at Talavera, a costly battle in which her son's regiment has, he believes, been virtually wiped out. In the third section, "The Vision of Sudden Death," he narrates an incident at night on the Manchester-to-Kendal mail in which the coachman nods off and, with De Quincey seemingly unable to seize the reins and take evasive action, the vehicle narrowly avoids collision with two lovers in an oncoming gig. It is only the young man in the gig who can avert disaster, and he responds with only seconds to spare. In the final section, the celebrated "Dream-Fugue," De Quincey tells the reader how the figure of that same terrified young woman, glimpsed for just a few moments, subsequently entered into the "gorgeous mosaics" of his dreams, featuring in a variety of perilous or fatal situations. In the final, apocalyptic, dream-sequence De Quincey's mail-coach becomes a "triumphal car" proceeding at supernatural pace down a cathedral aisle of infinite length; a female infant who temporarily obstructs its path somehow becomes synonymous with all the victims of war, past and present, while her apparent survival or exaltation stands not only for the material gains of "Waterloo and Recovered Christendom" but also for the spiritual end of resurrection and eternal life.

De Quincey mourned the passing of coach transport. He believed that trains had altered the rhythm of human life. "Out of pure blind sympathy with trains, men will begin to trot through the streets," he predicted, "and in the next generation, they will take to cantering." In his severe, though not humorless, judgement, "iron tubes and boilers have disconnected man's heart." One consequence of this revolution in transportation became apparent within decades of the publication of "The English Mail-Coach." The inns that had served the old system would not survive.

In *The Pickwick Papers*, which contains many wonderful nostalgic scenes of coach travel, Charles Dickens describes the state of the inns in London at the end of the coaching era:

> There are in London several old inns, once the headquarters of celebrated coaches in the days when coaches performed their journeys in a graver and more solemn manner than they do in these times; but which have now degenerated into little more than the abiding and booking places of country wagons. The reader would look in vain for any of these ancient hostelries, among the Golden Crosses and Bull and Mouths, which rear their stately fronts in the improved streets of London. If he would light upon any of these old places, he must direct his steps to the obscurer quarters of the town; and there in some secluded nooks he will find several, still standing with a kind of gloomy sturdiness, amidst the modern innovations which surround them.
>
> In the Borough especially, there still remain some half dozen old inns, which have preserved their external features unchanged, and which have escaped alike the rage for public improvement, and the encroachments of private speculation. Great, rambling, queer, old places they are, with galleries, and passages, and staircases, wide enough and antiquated enough, to furnish materials for a hundred ghost stories, supposing we should ever be reduced to the lamentable necessity of inventing any, and that the world should exist long enough to exhaust the innumerable veracious legends connected with old London Bridge, and its adjacent neighbourhood on the Surrey side.

Beginning in the 1870s developers began to tear down the coaching inns of London. The Tabard Inn was demolished in 1873. The Oxford Arms in Warwick Lane, near St Paul's Cathedral, was demolished in 1875. The King's Head in Southwark was demolished by 1885. The White Hart in Southwark was demolished in 1889. The list goes on and on.

Today the only surviving galleried coaching inn in London is The George. Even this is a partial survival. Only one of its three sides is still standing. The other two were pulled down by the Great Northern Railway Company in 1889 to build warehouses. These were later replaced with modernist constructions. But the one side that remains is perfectly preserved and is still a working pub.

For my own part I share Sir John Betjeman's love of railways but I think De Quincey makes a point well taken. The coach services were an economy and a society almost unto themselves. Passengers, coachmen, innkeepers, and tradesmen supported and linked together innumerable little communities across the country to an extent that no amount of efficiency can justify disrupting. But for all that the railway was a loud, smoking, violent shock to men and women of De Quincey's generation, it operated along similar principles to the old coach lines, employed a comparable number of people, and linked communities in a way that was harmonious with the needs of society, nature, and the landscape.The ideal transportation system is a hybrid incorporating a mix of different sustainable approaches. By the end of the Victorian period exactly such a system had been built. In his 1993 book, *The Geography of Nowhere*, James Howard Kunstler describes travel in upstate New York at the end of the nineteenth century and the beginning of the twentieth:

> There was a time just before the First World War when a person could get around this part of the world by train, trolley, boat, automobile, horse, or on foot, and in fact each mode of transportation had its place. This rich variety of possibilities is hard to imagine in our age, when the failure to own a car is tantamount to a failure

in citizenship, and our present transportation system is as much of a monoculture as our way of housing or farming. Factory workers walked or took the trolley across the Hudson. Shoppers walked to market. Stores delivered orders too big to carry. Freight moved long distance by rail or boat, and by truck or wagon only locally. Anybody who had urgent business with the greater world at large could hop on a train and get to Albany in an hour or New York City inside of five.

This lo-tech hybrid system could have continued indefinitely were it not for the leveraging of resources and government policy to make automobiles the primary—if not sole—mode of transportation throughout the developed world in the twentieth century. As late as the 1950s the system described by Kunstler could still be found in parts of Europe.

The American photographer Jack Birns crossed the Swiss Alps in 1950 to document one of the last stagecoach services in Europe, which ran between towns along the Simplon Pass. He had first encountered this survival from an earlier age six months prior while photographing a journey on the legendary Orient Express railway train for *LIFE* magazine. The iconic blue Wagon-Lits carriages of the Orient Express could travel through tunnels under the Simplon Pass in approximately twenty minutes while the stagecoaches took ten hours to go over them—but both modes of transportation were suited to their purpose. Stagecoaches served a vital function for the remote Alpine towns carrying passengers, mail, and supplies between them, as similar coaches had done for centuries.

I like to think that such a compromise would have been agreeable to De Quincey and his generation. As the reserves of cheap oil that fuel the present-day economy run out, it may yet be agreeable to a future generation.

11
Modern Origins of the Mystery Genre

I am an avid reader of mystery stories, particularly from that long golden age of English mysteries that ran from the nineteenth century until the mid-twentieth, when the genre was characterized by gentlemen detectives, period atmosphere, eccentricity, and strangeness, before the advent of American police procedurals and hardboiled prose. The literary "mystery" as we know it today began with the work of three writers in the early and middle decades of the nineteenth century. A line can be drawn from Thomas De Quincey (1785-1859) to Edgar Allan Poe (1809-1849) to Wilkie Collins (1824-1889), from them to Sir Arthur Conan Doyle (1859-1930), and from Doyle to all of the major mystery writers that came after.

De Quincy was born into a prosperous Manchester mercantile family in 1785. Upon the death of his father, control of his education and inheritance was entrusted to several guardians, who saw that he was furnished with a classical education. By the age of fifteen he had distinguished himself as a student at King Edward's School in Bath. "That boy," said one of the dons, "could harangue an Athenian mob better than you or I could address an English one." De Quincey was ready for higher education and hoped to go on to Oxford. In this ambition his guardians prevaricated, postponed, and generally stymied him. They sent him to continue his preparatory education at Manchester Grammar School where he was miserable. By nature he was a sensitive and melancholy young man. De Quincey resolved to run away from school and his guardians, which he did, just before his seventeenth birthday, relying on what little money he had in his possession, or could borrow, to make his way across the country. When this money ran out he took odd jobs to survive and could often afford only one small meal per day.

Eventually, De Quincey made his way to London. He was homeless at first, sleeping in the rough, unable to appeal to family acquaintances, for fear that his guardians would find him. He was given occasional crusts of bread by a man who took pity on him. With the onset of winter, the same man allowed him to stay in an unused house on Greek Street near Soho Square. This house was large, empty of furniture, and infested with rats. A neglected young girl also lived in the house, and De Quincey did his best to comfort and provide for her. De Quincey's benefactor was a lawyer of dubious character and practices: he moved around frequently and, when present, regarded anyone who appeared at the door with suspicion.

During the day, De Quincey sat in parks or on doorsteps, slowly wasting away from hunger and malnutrition. He got along amiably with the prostitutes in the area, which was, at the time, London's red light district. They protected him from the watchmen. One of these prostitutes, a fifteen year old girl named Ann, became his close friend and probably the love of his life. They spent most of their free time together, walking the streets or sitting in places of shelter. Ann was kind to De Quincey and tried to care for him. On one occasion, when he came near fainting from hunger, Ann spent her own meager resources to buy a cup of spiced wine to revive him. She told De Quincey about her past. She had been treated unjustly and he suggested that she might find restitution if she presented her case to a magistrate. He offered to help "avenge her on the brutal ruffian who had plundered her little property," but she was hesitant.

De Quincey was in desperate need of money, for himself, and now for Ann. He appealed to a Jewish moneylender who agreed to advance him a large sum on the condition that De Quincey's school friend, a young earl, stand as guarantor for the loan. De Quincey needed to travel to Eton to enlist the help of his friend. He had fortunately just received ten pounds from a family acquaintance. He gave a significant amount of this money to Ann, and used the rest to further his borrowing scheme.

Ann walked with De Quincey to Piccadilly, where he would catch the mail coach to Eton. As they sat together in a nearby square, De Quincey felt hopeful about his prospects and assured her of his intention to share whatever funds he was able to acquire with her. He told her he "would never forsake her as soon as [he] had power to protect her." Ann was nevertheless miserable. She hugged him and cried as they said goodbye. De Quincey expected his trip to take around a week, and so he made plans to meet Ann again when he returned. She agreed to wait for him at the bottom of Great Titchfield Street, which was their "customary haven," every night at six o'clock in the evening, beginning five days after his departure. Confident in this plan— after all, they had found each other every day for weeks without any more elaborate arrangements—De Quincey did not think to ask Ann her family name or address.

He set off on the journey to Eton, nearly falling from his place on top of the mail coach due to weakness and exhaustion. Arriving at last, he succeeded in finding his friend the Earl. Though he sat down with his friend to a lavish breakfast, better than any meal he had eaten for months, De Quincey found that he was hardly able to keep food down after so long without. His friend agreed to partially guarantee the loan, a compromise that the moneylender later rejected, and De Quincey returned to London earlier than expected, after only three days. He waited for Ann at their *rendezvous* point on Great Titchfield Street. When she did not appear after several days, he made inquiries about her and tried to trace her based on the vague information he had, such as the street (but not the house) where she lived. He could find no trace of her. It was as though she had disappeared.

De Quincey left London soon after, the loan having fallen through. Before departing, he gave his forwarding address to an acquaintance who had also known Ann. For a long time, he still hoped he might hear from her and find her again. He never did.

After attending Worcester College, Oxford, De Quincey moved to Grasmere in the Lake District, where he sought out the Lake Poets, Samuel Taylor Coleridge and William Wordsworth. He had read their *Lyrical Ballads* while still a student at King Edward's School and the poems had made a deep impression upon him. De Quincey quickly became a member of their circle; they mentored him, and he later contributed greatly to their reputations with a series of essays on their work. He married during this period, eventually fathering eight children, and lived for ten years at Dove Cottage, where Wordsworth had written his most famous poems.

By the late 1810s De Quincey had become a professional essayist and journalist in his own right. He was hired in 1818 as editor of *The Westmorland Gazette*, a Tory journal published in the Lake District. Like Coleridge, Wordsworth, the poet laureate Robert Southey, and other members of his circle, De Quincey was an avowed conservative. In *The Guardian*, James Purdon writes that De Quincey held, "reactionary views on the Peterloo massacre and the Sepoy rebellion;" he was against "Catholic emancipation and the enfranchisement of the common people." In personal correspondence, De Quincey "reserved 'Jacobin' as his highest term of opprobrium." Purdon calls him, "a fascist *avant la letter*." Hardly. He was, like Coleridge, a sensible Protestant Tory. Purdon quips, "Champagne socialists are so common as to be unremarkable; De Quincey was a laudanum Tory." Laudanum is a solution of opium dissolved in alcohol. This is an allusion to the circumstance with which De Quincey is most commonly associated: his lifelong dependence on the drug.

Although he lived to the age of seventy-four, De Quincey never physically recovered from the period of sustained, border-line starvation that he had suffered in London during his teenage years. His stomach had atrophied to the extent that he could hardly eat without being sick and recurring pain in his abdomen made it difficult to lie down. These problems were obviously exacerbated by the laudanum he began taking to treat them when he was nineteen years old.

In 1820 De Quincey published *Confessions of an English Opium Eater* which made him instantly famous—or infamous. The book detailed his ongoing and increasingly debilitating use of opium, being in part autobiography, in part a dispassionate record of self-medication and addiction, and in part a feat of remarkable self-analysis (De Quincey coined the term "subconscious" mind).

Portrait of Thomas De Quincey
by George Hamlin Fitch, circa 1851.

The *Confessions* called attention to the worrisome side effects of a drug that was sold over the counter by druggists and grocers at the time. It also made opium use into a romantic literary trope, popular with the Sensation and Decadent writers of the later nineteenth century. De Quincey's descriptions of the effect of opium on his dreams suggested recreational uses for the drug. He had been susceptible to unusually vivid dreams and nightmares even before he began taking it. Under the influence of laudanum his dreams became even more vivid and intense. Time seemed to warp. He had visions of a universe of beauty and horror. He suffered nightmares that felt as though they lasted for years. He described one unsettling dream in which, "upon the rocking waters of the ocean [a] human face began to appear;

the sea appeared paved with innumerable faces upturned to the heavens—faces imploring, wrathful, despairing, surged upwards by thousands, by myriads, by generations, by centuries: my agitation was infinite; my mind tossed and surged with the ocean." His dreams began to reflect the Oriental aesthetic associated with the drug. He wrote, in language redolent of Coleridge's *Kubla Khan*,

> I ran into pagodas, and was fixed for centuries at the summit or in secret rooms: I was the idol; I was the priest; I was worshipped; I was sacrificed. I fled from the wrath of Brama through all the forests of Asia: Vishnu hated me: Seeva laid wait for me. I came suddenly upon Isis and Osiris: I had done a deed, they said, which the ibis and the crocodile trembled at. I was buried for a thousand years in stone coffins, with mummies and sphinxes, in narrow chambers at the heart of eternal pyramids. I was kissed, with cancerous kisses, by crocodiles; and laid, confounded with all unutterable slimy things, amongst reeds and Nilotic mud.

Mystical and outré passages like these have always been the most popular part of the *Confessions*, which is otherwise a restrained and profoundly humane book. De Quincey emerged from the minor scandal that it provoked with a reputation as a writer of dark sensibilities. This was confirmed in 1827 when he published a piece of ink-black satire entitled, "On Murder Considered as one of the Fine Arts," in *Blackwood's Magazine*. It was this essay probably more than any other that inspired later writers of mystery fiction.

"On Murder" purports to be a lecture given to a gentleman's club whose members are connoisseurs of death. They appreciate killings that conform to Aristotle's theory of catharsis in drama. "The final purpose of murder," the lecturer says, "is precisely the same as that of tragedy in Aristotle's account of it; viz. 'to cleanse the heart by means of pity and terror.'" De Quincey wrote at length about the Ratcliffe Highway murders which occurred in Wapping, East London, in December of 1811. A sailor named John Williams slaughtered Timothy Marr, a shopkeeper, Marr's wife, infant son, apprentice, and servant girl in their home at night. A week later he did the same to John Williamson, proprietor of the King's Arms tavern, Williamson's wife, and servant. Williams was arrested for the crimes and hanged himself while in police custody.

De Quincey examined the details of these murders, calling attention to crime scene investigation and the identification of clues, themes crucial to the later development of the detective genre.

The fictional Society of Connoisseurs in Murder represents a foreshadowing of the modern mystery and detective genre, but the creation of that genre was the work of another author: Edgar Allan Poe.

Poe's character C. Auguste Dupin, a clear-thinking, puzzle-solving investigator even before the word "detective" came into common use, was the model for later characters in the genre. Dupin is the prototype of the gentleman detective: a scholar from a once wealthy family, now fallen on hard times, who conducts investigations, not as a professional, but with varied motives and in conjunction with the anonymous narrator of the tales in which he appears. Dupin is famous for his method, which Poe dubbed "ratiocination." He is a close observer of details and makes inferences through extreme rational and logical thinking. Dupin uses these skills to put himself in the minds of criminals, solving crimes by thinking from their point of view.

The first story in which Dupin appears, "The Murders in the Rue Morgue," was published in 1841. Dupin and his friend the narrator live together in Paris, and they become interested in newspaper accounts of the mysterious and gruesome murder of two women. When a former acquaintance of Dupin is arrested for the crime on only circumstantial evidence, Dupin steps forward to help. The clues have the police baffled: one body in a chimney and one outside the house, a murder scene in a locked room, tufts of non-human hair, and witness reports of two voices—one speaking an unintelligible language. Dupin infers from the super-human agility and strength of the murderer, and the tufts of hair, that the culprit is an orangutan. He proves this by tracking down the sailor who controls the beast.

Poe followed "Rue Morgue" with a second Dupin story a year later, "The Mystery of Marie Rogêt." This complex tale was based on the real-life murder of Mary Cecilia Rogers in New York City in 1838 and represents an attempt by Poe to solve the case. The third and final story in which Dupin is featured, "The Purloined Letter," was published in 1844. Here the police seek Dupin's help on a case where a Minister "D–" is blackmailing a woman with a revealing letter that "D–" has stolen. The police assume that "D–" must have the letter readily accessible, and they have thoroughly searched every potential hiding place in the hotel rooms where he is staying without success. A month later, after a huge reward is offered for the letter, the police return to visit Dupin, who produces the letter. He explains to the narrator that the police underestimated their opponent, who knew their methods and instead left the letter disguised in plain sight. Dupin, recognizing the letter even with its external alterations, arranged a distraction, took it, and left a decoy in its place. Poe called the story, "perhaps the best of my tales of ratiocination."

The Dupin stories were the direct model for Sir Arthur Conan Doyle's Sherlock Holmes stories. Holmes and Dupin use the same method of deductive and inferential reasoning to connect clues. Holmes, like Dupin, is a gentleman amateur. Holmes, like Dupin, is assisted by a friend and fellow lodger, Doctor Watson, who narrates the stories. In the first novel in which Holmes appears, *A Study in Scarlet*, Watson compares his method to that of Dupin. Holmes balks, "In my opinion, Dupin was a very inferior fellow...He had some analytical genius, no doubt; but he was by no means such a phenomenon as Poe appears to imagine." But Sir Arthur himself was well aware of the debt that he owed to Poe. "Each is a root from which a whole literature has developed," he said of the Dupin stories. "Where was the detective story until Poe breathed the breath of life into it?"

There is no doubt that Poe was influenced by De Quincey in the broadest sense. He read the English magazines in which De Quincey was published and expressed admiration for the *Confessions*. In a piece of humor that Poe composed for the *American Museum* in December of 1838, entitled, "How to Write a Blackwood's Article," he noted, "Then we have the *Confessions of an Opium Eater*—fine, very fine!—glorious imagination—acute speculation—plenty of fire and fury, and a good spicing of the decidedly unintelligible."

In at least one instance Poe was directly inspired by De Quincey. Poe's short story "The Masque of the Red Death" is based on an episode from De Quincey's novel *Klosterheim, or the Masque*. In her 1937 thesis, *The Influence of Thomas De Quincey on Edgar Allan Poe*, Ruth Kelly explains,

> The situation from *Klosterheim* which Poe borrowed for "The Masque of the Red Death" is a masqued ball found in Chapters XIV, XV, and XVI. A mysterious masked marauder has been bringing destruction and death of a bloody nature throughout the country. It has been impossible to apprehend him, and the country is stricken with fear. The prince consequently barricades the castle during a great masqued ball to which he has issued twelve hundred invitations. A challenge of defiance has been hurled at the "Masque," as the invader is called. Feeling runs high. Midnight approaches. A whisper begins to circulate that an alien presence is in the room. The whisper grows into a buzz. The music ceases abruptly. The order to seize him is given. The "Masque" discloses his identity to the prince who cries out and falls full length upon the ground bereft of consciousness. All rush toward the "Masque" in order to seize him, but in the confusion he disappears.

Poe built upon this premise, and transformed it, making the masked figure an allegory for plague in his own story. But it is clear that he read De Quincey closely and borrowed from him. In turn, Wilkie Collins read, and borrowed from, both of them. If Poe wrote the first detective stories, Wilkie Collins wrote the first modern mystery novels. T.S. Eliot famously praised *The Moonstone* as "the first, the longest, and the best of modern English detective novels." Collins drew on the earlier gothic tradition but also on the new literary strands being teased out of that tradition by De Quincey and Poe.

In Collins's 1859 novel, *The Woman in White*, a young artist, Walter Hartright, takes a position as drawing master for two young half-sisters who live with their uncle at a manor house in Cumberland. One night before he leaves London to begin his employment, he encounters a distressed woman dressed entirely in white and helps her; later he learns that she escaped from an insane asylum. In Cumberland, Walter and his student, Laura Fairlie, fall in love. She bears an uncanny resemblance to the woman in white, whose name is Anne Catherick. However, Laura is engaged to another man, Sir Percival Glyde, and marries him. When the couple returns from the honeymoon, Laura's half-sister Marian discovers that Sir Percival is in financial trouble. Since Laura has refused to sign over her marriage settlement, Glyde and his friend, Count Fosco, are planning to take Laura's money by other means.

At the same time, the terminally ill Anne promises to share a secret with Laura that could ruin Glyde. Before she can do so, Fosco and Glyde carry out their plan, switching the identities of Laura and Anne. Laura is drugged and sent to the asylum, and Anne dies and is buried as Laura—leaving Laura's money to Glyde. Fortunately, Marian finds and rescues Laura. They live in poverty in London with Walter until, at last, they discover Glyde's secret and find a way to re-establish Laura's identity, restoring their fortunes.

Collins's 1868 novel *The Moonstone* concerns the theft of a large diamond that a British officer has brought from India and bequeathed to his niece, Rachel. The diamond is taken from Rachel's room on the evening of her birthday, after she wore it to a party. Suspects abound: three Indian jugglers are in the vicinity; a maid, Rosanna Spearman, acts suspiciously; Rachel refuses to let the police search her room and spurns the man with whom she was in love, Franklin Blake.

During the following year, Blake leaves England. Rachel accepts the proposal of another man who was at the party, the philanthropist Godfrey Ablewhite, but later breaks the engagement. When Blake returns, he discovers that Rosanna was in love with him. She found stains on his clothes from the wet paint on Rachel's door and tried to cover for his assumed crime, eventually killing herself in despair. He then confronts Rachel, who tells him that she saw him take the stone. Blake is entirely confused, but with the help of a doctor's assistant, and a probing, clever police detective, Sergeant Cuff, he pieces together that he had been drugged with opium on the night of the robbery. In a trance, Blake took the Moonstone from Rachel's room to protect it, with no memory of the event, and no memory of where he put it.

Franklin and Rachel learn that the stone is in a bank, pledged to a moneylender. They watch the bank to see who will redeem the diamond, and follow this line of investigation to the discovery of Godfrey Ablewhite's body. He has been murdered and the stone stolen again. They realize that Godfrey, on the brink of financial ruin, took the diamond from the drugged and sleepwalking Blake on the night it disappeared. Godfrey was murdered by the three Indians—in fact Brahmin priests in disguise—who return the stone to its rightful place on the statue of a moon god in India.

The influence of Poe on Collins is subtle but pervasive. In a review of Collins's novel *After Dark*, George Eliot made a connection between the two authors, writing, "Edgar Poe's tales were an effort of genius to reconcile the two tendencies—to appal the imagination yet satisfy the intellect, and Mr. Wilkie Collins in this respect often follows in Poe's tracks." A.B. Emrys identifies Collins as,

> the bridging figure between Poe and Conan Doyle, but not because of Sergeant Cuff. Not only did Collins reprise plot from Poe multiple times but the influence of Poe's prose monologues is a key factor in Collins's successful development of the casebook form. The vivid voices of *The Woman in White* and *The Moonstone* are central to the continued popularity of these novels and their being ranked as Collins's best works, and their dramatic monologues are built on those of Poe's criminals.

"He opened the bedroom door, and went out"
(Illustration for The Moonstone) by John Sloan, 1908.

The influence of De Quincey is more specific. The plot twist involving opium in *The Moonstone* hinges upon the *Confessions*. "There," the doctor's assistant tells Blake, handing him a book, "are the far-famed *Confessions of an English Opium Eater*! Take the book away with you and read it." Episodes from De Quincey's memoir, creatively interpreted by Collins, provide an explanation for the goings on in *The Moonstone*.

In 1887 Doyle published *A Study in Scarlet*. He would go on to write a total of four novels and fifty-six short stories featuring Sherlock Holmes over a period ending in 1927. Throughout this canon of work, references, not just to Poe, but to De Quincey and Collins, appear. We know that Doyle read "On Murder." In his short story "The Silver Hatchet," he describes the mood in Budapest, where a series of murders have been committed with the titular object: "The only parallel to this intense feeling was to be found in our own country at the time of the Williams murders described by De Quincey." The Ratcliffe Highway murders are alluded to again in *A Study in Scarlet*, where they are compared to the "Brixton Mystery" in a fictional article from *The Daily Telegraph*. We also know that Doyle was familiar with the *Confessions*. He seems to have been inspired by his reading of De Quincey to give Holmes a drug habit. In "A Scandal in Bohemia," Watson notices that Holmes has "risen out of his drug-created dreams," a concept taken straight from the *Confessions*, "and was hot upon the scent of some new problem." Watson, as a disapproving physician, describes another character's addiction to opium in "The Man With the Twisted Lip." Here, the doctor observes, "The habit grew upon him, as I understand, from some foolish freak when he was at college; for having read De Quincey's description of his dreams and sensations, he had drenched his tobacco with laudanum to produce the same results."

Likewise, plot elements from the novels of Wilkie Collins echo through the Holmes canon. As Charles Rzepka notes, "The plundered Moonstone inspired Doyle's choice of the Agra treasure as incentive to crime in the Holmes novella, *The Sign of Four*, where the three Brahmins that Collins set in pursuit of the gem reappear as three Muslim and Sikh conspirators who seize the treasure during the height of the Mutiny." Doyle had already written an homage to *The Moonstone*: his early novel, *The Mystery of Cloomber*. In that book three vengeful Buddhist priests take the place of the three Brahmins.

The Sherlock Holmes series was the wellspring of the whole modern mystery genre. But it too had its source in earlier works. Without De Quincey, Poe, and Collins there might have been no Holmes. And no genre.

Someone in the art department at Universal Pictures seems to have recognized that fact. There is a reference to De Quincey in the 1945 film *The House of Fear*. This was the tenth film in the long-running series with Basil Rathbone and Nigel Bruce as Holmes and Watson. The screenplay is an original story very loosely based on "The Adventure of the Five Orange Pips." In the film, Holmes and Watson are summoned to a remote castle in Scotland where seven men live together under a strange agreement by which they benefit from each other's life insurance policies. Someone is murdering them one by one.

While searching for clues Holmes inspects the volumes on a bookshelf, selecting one titled *Murder As a Fine Art*.

12
The Symbolist
ᏝManifesto

Most English-language readers will have at least a passing familiarity with the French writers who followed Baudelaire: Huysmans, Verlaine, Rimbaud, Mallarmé, Barbey d'Aurevilly. Rarely mentioned, however, is the name of Jean Moréas. Except for a few poems he has remained little-translated and little-known in the Anglophone world, despite his important legacy as the founder of the Symbolism movement.

Jean Moréas (1856-1910) was born Ioannis Papadiamantopoulos in Athens, Greece, to a distinguished family with ties to the Greek War of Independence—his grandfather helped raise the Christian flag at Agia Lavra in 1821, triggering the revolt against the Turks, and later died with Lord Byron at Missolonghi. His father served as attorney general to the high court of Athens and other relatives occupied important positions in the military, with one cousin appointed to the king's honor guard.

Moréas was educated in French by a Parisian governess who had formerly acted with the Comédie-Français, and he spent some of his childhood and adolescence in Marseilles. Precocious in his youth, he acquired a library of more than 2,000 books with an emphasis on Renaissance poetry and French literature. By age ten he had declared his aspiration to become the greatest of French poets.

Moréas reached Paris between 1875 and 1878. He had first been sent to Heidelberg to train as a lawyer. "My father wanted me in Germany," he would later tell friends. "I wanted to see France. Twice I fled my home and was able to reach Paris. Fate showed me the way—my star guiding me." At the age of 22 he settled in Paris permanently and began to establish himself as a writer. His first association was with the Hydropathes circle and he published extensively in their newspaper, *Le Chat Noir.*

In France at the *fin de siècle* the literary world was dominated by two forces. On the one hand: Emile Zola and the "Naturalists" who sought to render human experience in evolutionary terms—man impelled by "nerves and blood." On the other: that late-Romantic movement which had begun with Charles Baudelaire and his reading of Edgar Allan Poe, and which was later represented by Joris-Karl Huysmans and Stéphane Mallarmé, insisting cryptically upon higher realms of order and the intrusion of divine or satanic symbols in everyday life.

Moréas belonged resolutely to this latter camp, then known as Decadence. He saw implicit in its doctrine the teaching of the Neoplatonists that earthly forms were derived from heavenly models. Moréas believed that employing symbols from the sensible world, poets could evoke, by reflection, a higher one. Baudelaire had suggested much the same in his poem "Correspondences":

> In Nature's temple living pillars rise
> And words are murmured none have understood
> And man passes through a forest of symbols
> Watching him with friendly eyes
> Perfumes, colors and sounds correspond to one another
> Like long echoes which from afar merge into
> A deep and dark whole.

With the publication of *Les Syrtes* (1884) and *Les Cantilènes* (1886), his first major collections, Moréas became an apologist for the Decadent movement. Writing in publications like *Le Figaro* and *XIXe Siècle* he addressed critics who alleged superficiality, insisting that the movement was dedicated to the pursuit of higher truths. "Those who call themselves Decadents," he wrote in reply to the critic Paul Bourde, "seek above all in their art the pure Concept and the eternal Symbol."

Moréas was not interested in the aesthetic of moral despair that permeated Decadent literature. By identifying Baudelaire's legacy instead with an aspiration toward the divine, Moréas was preparing the way for a rejection of the "Decadent" label altogether. In *Le Figaro* of 18 September 1886 Moréas published the manifesto of Symbolism, a new movement that would appropriate the Decadents but purify and refocus their imagery. Here he emphasized the esoteric doctrine at its core:

> Symbolist poets seek to clothe the Idea in a tangible form, which would not be an end in itself, but which would remain subject to the Idea, while serving to express it. In its turn, the Idea must in no way allow itself to be deprived of the sumptuous robes of external analogies; for the essential characteristic of Symbolist art resides in never going as far as to reproduce the Idea in itself. So, in this art form, scenes of nature, human actions, all concrete phenomena, will not be depicted as such: they are tangible forms, whose purpose is to represent their concealed affinities with primordial Ideas.

In the wake of Symbolism, Moréas became a literary celebrity and a principal French poet. Among the young writers who followed him, he commanded something akin to adoration. (Oscar Wilde, dining in Paris with Moréas and his acolytes, stormed out of the restaurant in exasperation when they recited nothing but odes to Jean Moréas.) In temperament, he possessed a distance that often made him appear humorless, egotistical, or contemptuous. He could be harsh, but never vindictive or unfair. He was nocturnal, but morally upright, and absolutely restless. He would hold court in the cafés of Les Halles, sometimes passing through half a dozen in one night. The American critic Vance Thompson, who encountered Moréas at the Café François Premiére, described his entrance in "a long, monkish great-coat reaching his heels, a silk hat tipped over his eyebrows. His mustache is twisted up truculently. He has the air of Bobadil, of Drawcansir—of a pirate of the Spanish Main. Across his face runs a sneer like a sabre-cut. He stalks sombrely, a monocle glued in his right eye—which is absurd—and takes a seat in Verlaine's old corner."

Within a few years, Symbolism had become a broad, multi-disciplined school, encompassing visual art and music as well as literature. But increasingly, it was fueled by ideologies quite divergent from that of its founder. What frustrated Moréas about many of the new poets who flocked to Symbolism was their adoption of free verse, a technique that he had ironically championed himself in the manifesto. It is likely that as Moréas became more concerned with metaphysics, he came to see the undisciplined style at odds with the Platonic notion of a correct—or ideal—structure for which the artist should strive. There was a political dimension here as well. The faction that embraced free verse was increasingly tied to the political Left. The poet Adolphe Retté would declare this affinity in an article for *La Plume* in which he wrote, "two ideas have continued their evolution upward and have affirmed their vitality: in literature, free verse, in philosophy, the anarchist doctrine."

This trend was unacceptable to Moréas, who was a man of the Right. Although he remained publicly aloof from French politics, in private he was an ardent monarchist who felt even the Orleanist model of a "Citizen King" did not go far enough. One of his earliest supporters and friends was the classical critic Charles Maurras who founded the monarchist political faction, *Action Française*.

By 1890, Moréas had announced the demise of Symbolism—or, rather, its need of further clarification. This he provided with a new book of poetry, *Le Pèlerin Passionné*, and a new manifesto in *Le Figaro*. Aided by Maurras, Raymond de la Tailhède, Maurice du Plessis, and Ernest Raynaud, Moréas founded the *École Romane*. Their aim was to re-establish a traditional French poetry based on Medieval verse structure and Greco-Roman symbolism—a fitting synthesis for the Greek émigré, but one also rooted in traditional French mythology. (Whereas the Romans were said to descend from the Trojan Aeneas, the French claimed the Trojan Francus as their founding father.)

Charles Maurras probably deserves more credit for the

doctrine of Romanism than he is given. Much is made of the influence of Moréas and the *École Romane*—with its enchanted Medievalism—on Maurras and *Action Française*. But the influence went both ways. Maurras had long been a supporter of the *félibrige* writers in his native Provence—Frédéric Mistral and others—who promoted Occitan, the ancient vernacular form of Latin still spoken in the region. René Wellek, in *Yale French Studies*, writes that Maurras was "convinced of the possibility of a Provençal Renaissance, linguistic and poetic. Provence provided him with the symbolic center of Latinity: the crossroads of the Greek, Latin, and French traditions." A similar spirit animated the *École Romane*.

Soyez Symboliste (Portrait of Jean Moréas) by Paul Gauguin, 1891.

To many at the time, the rejection of Symbolism by its founder was jarring. The critic Max Nordau wrote that, "Moréas is one of the inventors of the word 'Symbolism.' For some few years he was the high-priest of this secret doctrine, and administered the duties of his service with requisite seriousness. One day he suddenly abjured his self-founded faith, and declared that

'Symbolism' had always been meant only as a joke, to lead fools by the nose withal; and that the true salvation of poetry was in Romanism."

The shift was nothing so dramatic. If anything, the *École Romane* presented a sharpening of the Symbolist philosophy. In his earlier manifesto, Moréas advocated a classical conception of symbol; now he was going a step further, advocating a return to actual classical symbols and structure. Indeed, the two major collections Moréas published under the aegis of the Roman school—*Le Pèlerin Passionné* (1891) and *Les Stances* (1893)—come across as natural developments of his work to date.

Moréas would no doubt have been pleased to know that these latter volumes, his greatest successes at the time, remain the ones for which he is best remembered. And yet, as biographer John Davis Butler laments, even in France Moréas is "received by the public, *le public vulgaire*, with a casualness akin to apathy."

The Manifesto

As an addendum to my profile of Jean Moréas, I offer an English-language translation of his essay, "The Symbolist Manifesto," which was first published in *Le Figaro* on September 18, 1886:

> As with all the arts, literature is constantly evolving: a cyclical process characterized by a pre-established looking back to the past which must also take into account various factors related to the march of time and a changing social structure. It would be unnecessary to note that each new development in the artistic evolutionary process follows directly on from the descent into decrepitude, the inevitable demise of the immediately preceding school of thought. Two examples will suffice: that of Ronsard triumphing over the paltry efforts of Marot's final imitators, and that of the Romantic school proclaiming its victory over a classicism whose ruins Baour Lormian and Etienne de

Jouy had failed to return to its former glory. The truth is that all art carries within itself the seeds of its own fall from grace and ultimate destruction; thus from copy to copy, from imitation to imitation, that which bloomed with the freshness and vigor of youth is destined to wither and shrivel into old age; that which gleamed new and spontaneous cannot help but become clichéd and commonplace.

So it is with the Romantics, who after having set off all the jangling alarm bells of revolt, after their days of glorious battles, lost their strength and their grace, gave up their daring acts of heroism, and fell back into line, more doubting and wiser men. The movement vainly hoped to rise again with the honorable and petty attempt of the Parnassians, then finally conceded defeat, like a king in his dotage, allowing itself to be deposed by Naturalism, to which we cannot seriously attribute any value other than that of legitimate protest, albeit ill-advised, against the dreariness of the few writers in fashion at the time.

Thus the time was ripe for a new form of art. This necessary inevitability, a long time in the bud, has just come into flower. And all the ineffective jokes of our paragons of the press, all those concerns of the serious critics, all the bad temper of a public roused out of their slavish indifference, only serve as a daily reaffirmation of the vitality of the current evolution in French literature, this evolution that hasty judges, through an inexplicable antinomy, termed Decadence. Let us note however that Decadent literature shows itself to be essentially tough and fibrous, timid and servile: all Voltaire's tragedies for example bear these blemishes of Decadence. And what can be reproached, what can *we* reproach this new school of? An excess of pomp, the strangeness of the metaphor, a new vocabulary in which harmonies mingle with line and color: these are the characteristics of any Renaissance.

We have already suggested the term *Symbolism* as being the only one capable of properly representing the current trend of the creative spirit in art.

This term may be adopted.

It was mentioned at the beginning of this article that evolution in art goes in cycles which are greatly complicated by divergence from them; thus, in order to trace the exact ancestry of the new school, it is necessary to go back to certain of Alfred de Vigny's poems, to Shakespeare, to the mystics, and still further back in time. A vast number of words would be needed to address these considerations; let us merely say that Charles Baudelaire should be regarded as the true father of the current movement; Mr Stéphane Mallarmé imbued it with a sense of mystery and wonder; in its honor Mr Paul Verlaine broke the cruel shackles of verse form that the prestigious pen of Mr Théodore de Banville had previously succeeded in bending. *Le Suprême Enchantement* has not yet been achieved. Those who have just arrived will be confronted with a stubborn and jealous task.

Enemies of teaching, of declamation, of false sensibility, and of objective description, the Symbolist poets seek to clothe the Idea in a tangible form, which would nonetheless not be an end in itself, but which would remain subject to the Idea, while serving to express it. In its turn, the Idea must in no way allow itself to be deprived of the sumptuous robes of external analogies; for the essential characteristic of Symbolist art resides in never going as far as to reproduce the Idea in itself. So, in this art form, scenes of nature, human actions, all concrete phenomena, will not be depicted as such: they are tangible forms, whose purpose is to represent their concealed affinities with primordial Ideas.

The accusation of obscurity hurled at this aesthetic by desultory readers should not surprise us. But what can be done about it? *The Pythians* of Pindar, Shakespeare's *Hamlet,* Dante's *Vita Nuova, Part Two* of Goethe's *Faust, La Tentation de St Antoine* of Flaubert—were they not also accused of obscurity?

For the exact synthesis of Symbolism to be rendered accurately, it requires an archetypal, complex style: pure words, one phrase acting as a buttress and alternating with another of undulating decline, meaningful pleonasms, mysterious ellipses, the anacoluthon left in suspense, every trope bold and multifaceted: in short, good French—revitalized and modernized—that good, luxuriant, and spirited French language of before the likes of Vaugelas and Boileau-Despréaux, the language of François Rabelais and Philippe de Commines, of Villon and Rutebeuf, and of so many other writers, who were free and did not flinch from throwing their linguistic barbs, just as the Thracian archers threw their sinuous arrows.

RHYTHM: the ancient meters revived, disorder skillfully transformed into order, incandescent rhyme beaten out like a shield of gold and bronze, taking its place beside rhymes of abstruse fluidity; the alexandrine with its many mobile pauses; the use of certain odd numbers.

Here I crave your indulgence in asking you to pay heed to my little **INTERLUDE**, drawn from a gem of a book, *Le Traité de Poésie Française* [the *Little Treatise on French Poetry*], in which Mr Théodore de Banville re-creates the pitiless judgment of the god at Claros, causing many a Midas to grow a pair of monstrous ass's ears on their head.

Your attention please!

The characters of the play are as follows:

1. A DETRACTOR OF THE SYMBOLIST SCHOOL
2. THEODORE DE BANVILLE
3. ERATO

Scene I

THE DETRACTOR: Oh! These Decadents! What pomposity! What gibberish! How true the words of our great Molière when he wrote:
"That figurative style where all is vanity / Taking no account of good nature or truth."

THEODORE DE BANVILLE: Our great Molière may here be blamed for penning a bad couplet which itself takes as little account as possible of good nature. Of what good nature? Of what truth? An apparent disorder, a flamboyant madness, an impassioned pomposity; these are the very essence of lyric poetry. To go to the extremes of figure and color is not such a bad thing and this is not what will cause our literature to perish. In its darkest hour, when it expires absolutely, as during the First French Empire for example, it is not pomposity or an excess of ornament that sounds its death knell, it is dullness. Excellent as good taste and naturalness may be, they are assuredly less useful to poetry than we may believe. Shakespeare's *Romeo and Juliet* is written from beginning to end in a style as affected as that of the Marquis of Mascarill; while the most felicitous and natural simplicity shines through Ducis's adaptation of it.

THE DETRACTOR: But the caesura, the caesura! They are violating the caesura!!

THEODORE DE BANVILLE: In his remarkable prosody published in 1844, Mr Wilhem Tenint established that the alexandrine recognizes twelve different combinations, starting with the line which has its caesura after the first syllable and ending with that which has its caesura after the eleventh syllable. In other words, the truth is that the caesura may be placed after any syllable in alexandrine verse. Similarly, he established that lines of six, seven, eight, nine, or ten syllables recognize variable and differently placed caesurae. Let us go further; let us dare to declare complete freedom and say that it is by ear alone that these complex considerations can be judged. We have always perished through lack of courage, not by its excess.

THE DETRACTOR: Unspeakable! Not to respect the alternance of rhymes! Sir, are you not aware that the Decadents dare to take liberties with the hiatus! I say even the hi-a-tus!!

THEODORE DE BANVILLE: The hiatus, the syllabic diphthong in a line of verse, all the rest of those forbidden things, and especially the optional use of masculine or feminine rhymes, gave the poet of genius an immense and inexhaustible supply of delicate effects, ever varied and unexpected. But one had to be a poet of genius, as well as possessing a musical ear, to be able to handle this complex and scholarly verse form, whereas fixed rules, if followed to the letter, alas, allow the most mediocre writers to write *passable poetry!* Who therefore has benefited from the regulation of poetry? Mediocre poets only!

THE DETRACTOR: But what of the Romantic revolution?

THEODORE DE BANVILLE: The Romantic revolution was left unfinished. What a tragedy that Victor Hugo, that victorious Hercules with hands dripping with blood, lacked complete revolutionary fervor and so spared some of the monsters he had been charged to exterminate with flaming arrows!

THE DETRACTOR: All reform is foolishness! Emulation of Victor Hugo: that is where the salvation of French poetry lies!

THEODORE DE BANVILLE; When Hugo unfettered verse form, it may have been believed that those poets who followed him, taking example from him, would aspire to be free and only accountable to themselves. But such is our love of servitude that the new poets vied with each other in copying and imitating Hugo's most used forms, combinations and rhythms, instead of searching for new ones. Thus, bred for the yoke, we went from one form of slavery to another and after the *Classical platitudes,* we were given the *Romantic platitudes:* hackneyed in rhythm, in words and in rhyme; and these platitudes, that is to say the commonplace made chronic, toll the death knell in poetry as in all else. On the contrary, let us dare to be alive! And being alive signifies breathing the fresh air rather than our neighbor's breath, even if our neighbor be God Himself!

Scene II

ERATO (*invisible*): Your *Little Treatise on French Poetry* is a delightful work, Master Banville. But young poets are up to their eyes in blood, battling against those *monsters* nourished by Nicolas Boileau; Master Banville, pray be quiet, you are being summoned to the battlefield!

THEODORE DE BANVILLE (*dreamily*): Curses! Could it be that I have failed in my duty as the eldest and as a lyric poet?

(The author of *Les Exilées* breathes a dreadful sigh signifying the end of the interlude).

PROSE: novels, short stories, tales, fantasies,— evolve in a similar way to poetry. Elements which appear unrelated converge therein. Stendhal brings to it his translucent psychology, Balzac his keen observation of detail, Flaubert the rhythm of his vast soaring sentences, Mr Edmond de Goncourt his modern suggestive impressionism.

The concept of the Symbolist novel is polymorphous: sometimes a unique character moves around in surroundings distorted by his own hallucinations, by his own disposition: in this distortion lies the only *reality*. Shadowy figures with mechanical gestures flit around this unique character: they are merely a pretext for expressing his sensations and for conjecture. The character himself is a tragic mask or a buffoon, albeit perfectly human, while being doted with rationality. Sometimes the throng, superficially affected by what is going on around it, moves inexorably on, now jostling, now stagnant, towards acts which remain unfinished. Sometimes individual *wills* manifest themselves;

they are drawn to each other, cohere, and spread out towards a goal which, whether reached or thwarted, breaks them apart into their original elements. And at yet other times mythical phantasms, from the primordial Demogorgon to Belial, from the mystic poems of Kabir to the Nigromans, appear sumptuously adorned on Caliban's rock or in Titania's forest in the mixolydian mode of barbitons and octocordes.

As for Mr Zola, thus disdainful of the puerile Method of Naturalism, he was saved by a marvelous writer's instinct—the symbolic novel was built on the foundations of *subjective distortion,* based on the axiom: let art have no aim other than that of a simple, extremely succinct, point of departure.

JEAN MORÉAS

13

A Paean for Arthur Machen

Arthur Llewelyn Jones-Machen was born in Caerleon, Wales in March of 1863 to the Anglican clergyman John Edward Jones and his wife, Janet. The shortened form of Machen, which Arthur used for most of his life, was a surname from his mother's side of the family. He grew up in Llanddewi Fach, a rural parish outside of Caerleon, where his father was vicar. The area had a rich history intertwined with Welsh myth and folklore. The earliest legends of King Arthur placed the seat of his kingdom not in Camelot but in Caerleon. The landscape would influence Machen's future work in fantasy and weird fiction.

In the 1870s, archaeologists began to uncover remnants of Roman settlements in the region: stonework and pagan idols. Machen's own grandfather, who had been the vicar of Caerleon, was a well-regarded local antiquary, who had discovered Roman stones in his own churchyard. The sense that strangeness and the supernatural permeated the very land would remain with Machen. That countryside with its Roman ruins and fairy glens would reoccur often in his fiction. Much later, he wrote:

> I shall always esteem it as the greatest piece of fortune that has fallen to me, that I was born in that noble, fallen Caerleon-on-Usk, in the heart of Gwent.... For the older I grow the more firmly I am convinced that anything which I may have accomplished in literature is due to the fact that when my eyes were first opened in earliest

childhood they had before them the vision of an enchanted land.

As a boy, Machen was intelligent, reserved, and solitary. Fred Hando, in his volume of local history, *The Pleasant Land of Gwent*, attributes Machen's interest in the occult to an article about alchemy that he read in an old issue of Charles Dickens's magazine, *Household Words*, when he was eight years old. Hando elaborates on Machen's youthful reading habits: "He bought De Quincey's *Confessions of an English Opium Eater* at Pontypool Road Railway Station, *The Arabian Nights* at Hereford Railway Station, and borrowed *Don Quixote* from Mrs. Gwyn, of Llanfrechfa Rectory. In his father's library he found also the *Waverley Novels*, a three-volume edition of the *Glossary of Gothic Architecture*, and an early volume of Tennyson." By the time he was sent to study at Hereford Cathedral School at the age of eleven, he showed an interest in history and literature. His family might have sent him on to Oxford, where his father had studied, but they lacked the resources. Instead, he decided to pursue a career in journalism.

Machen moved to London in the early 1880s. He did not immediately attempt to establish himself in Fleet Street. Instead he lived on little and spent his time wandering and exploring the city. He observed the strange juxtaposition of old and new, as Victorian development encroached upon the often dilapidated remains of ancient London.

In 1881, shortly before moving to London, he published *Eleusinia*, a poetic treatment of the Greco-Roman mystery cult. He published his second book, *The Anatomy of Tobacco*, in 1884. This was a whimsical appreciation of pipe-smoking. Through his publisher, George Redway, Machen was hired as an editor at the magazine *Walford's Antiquarian*. During this period he undertook several translations from French literature, including a multi-volume edition of Casanova's *Memoirs*, and produced his first novel, *The Chronicle of Clemendy*.

In 1887, at the age of twenty-four, Machen married a young music teacher named Amy Hogg. His father died the same year, leaving an inheritance that allowed Machen to write full time. He had developed his mature style of prose by the end of the decade. His writing reflected a sense of nostalgia and an interest in supernatural and occult themes. His first major achievement was a short novel, *The Great God Pan*, for which he is still best known. The story, about a woman born of pagan ritual and occult science, caused a stir with its suggested horrors and perverse sexuality. *The Great God Pan* was published by John Lane in 1890 as part of the "Keynotes" series. It marked Machen's arrival as an associate of the literary Decadent movement. He became acquainted with other major figures of the genre, including Oscar Wilde and Aubrey Beardsley. He and Amy were living in a cottage in the Chilterns in southeast England. There he wrote another book, *The Three Imposters*, which was also published by Lane. It is a portmanteau novel which follows two bohemian friends as they try to learn the identity of a young man in spectacles who was seen throwing a Roman coin—"the gold Tiberius"—into the street as he ran terrified into the night. Along the way they hear many strange stories.

Machen's rise in the literary world was cut short by a scandal that did not involve him. The Decadent Movement was widely repudiated in the mid-1890s when Oscar Wilde was put on trial for sodomy and gross indecency. Machen continued to write over the next decade but did not publish. Fortunately, he still had his inheritance to live on. He wrote two novellas, *The White People* and *A Fragment of Life*, both of which evoked the mystical Welsh countryside of his childhood, as well as a novel, *The Hill of Dreams*, during this period. He also wrote a series of prose poems, which were later collected in *Ornaments of Jade*. In addition to writing, Machen took an editorial position at the magazine *Literature* in 1898. Though he did not remain there long, he had the opportunity to develop his own ideas on the subject of literary theory, which he outlined in the book, *Hieroglyphics*, in 1902.

The Hill of Dreams, which was written between 1895 and 1897, but not published until 1907, was his last word on the Decadent genre. It is widely regarded as his finest work, a judgment that he did not dispute. Machen told the writer E.H. Visiak, "I should think that on the whole *The Hill of Dreams* is my most successful experiment in literature." An annotated bibliography prepared by The Friends of Arthur Machen describes the haunting and ambiguous story as follows:

> Lucian Taylor, the hero, is damned, either through contact with an erotically pagan 'other' world or through something degenerate in his own nature, which he thinks of as a 'faun'. He becomes a writer, and when he moves to London he becomes trapped by the increasing reality of the dark imaginings of this creature within him, which become increasingly real. Machen drew copiously on his own early years in Wales and London, and the book as a whole is an exploration through imagination of a potential fate which he personally avoided. One of the first explorations in fiction of the figure of the doomed artist, who is biographically so much a part of the decadent 1890s.

As the turn of the twentieth century approached, Machen suffered a terrible loss. After a long illness, his wife, Amy, died of cancer in 1899. Machen was overwhelmed with grief and suffered a nervous breakdown. Friends encouraged him to recover by cultivating his spiritual life. Through Arthur Edward Waite, he joined the occult society, the Hermetic Order of the Golden Dawn. Though Machen shared the group's interest in the Western Mystery Tradition his own spiritual awakening was leading him in a different direction.

Machen was a lifelong Anglican Christian. Following the death of his wife, he experienced a religious epiphany. He would later write that during the "autumn of 1899-1900 . . . the two worlds of sense and spirit were admirably and wonderfully mingled, so that it was difficult, or rather impossible, to distinguish the outward and sensible glow from the inward and spiritual grace." He was a high churchman who favored the catholic inheritance of the Church of England over the reformed inheritance. But he identified the catholicity of Anglicanism with a Celtic Christianity that predated the arrival of missionaries from the Church of Rome.

He found other ways to work through the heartbreak of Amy's death as well. In 1901, he made the perhaps unexpected—but to anyone who knows the healing power of theater, not surprising—decision to become an actor. He joined Frederick Benson's theater company. Touring and performing gave Machen a source of optimism and confidence, which spilled over into the rest of his life. Though previously extremely reserved, he now became more outgoing and gregarious.

Four years after Amy's death, Machen married for a second time, to Dorothie Purefoy Hudleston. Purefoy, as she was called, was a fellow member of Benson's company. The couple frequently toured with the troupe and enjoyed a bohemian lifestyle. Purefoy encouraged Machen in both his faith and his writing. In 1906, at last, he published a collection of old and new pieces, *The House of Souls*. The following year, he published his masterwork of literary Decadence, *The Hill of Dreams*. However, the times had changed, as had Machen himself. He largely abandoned the themes of paganism and evil that had characterized his works of the *fin de siècle*.

A new theme appeared in his writings from the early 1900s onward. His interest in Celtic Christianity and mysticism came to define his work. He began to write for *The Academy*, a literary journal run by Lord Alfred Douglas, in which Machen explored the legends of King Arthur and the Holy Grail, placing them in the context of Celtic Christianity. Machen's writings on religion emphasized ritual and the imagination. During this time, he translated his interest in the Holy Grail to fiction in the novel, *The Secret Glory*, about a young orphan who achieves salvation and martyrdom on a modern quest for the Grail.

Toward the end of the decade, Machen ran into financial difficulties. To make ends meet, he returned to a career in journalism. He joined the staff of the *Daily Mail* in 1908 then transferred to *The Evening News* in 1910. As an experienced writer, he was asked to report on a variety of important subjects, including the funeral of renowned explorer Captain Robert Falcon Scott. Most of his regular pieces, however, focused on religion or on the arts. Though *The Evening News* offered Machen a good, reliable income, he chaffed at the constraints of full-time employment.

Despite his dissatisfaction with the job, it gave him his first real taste of fame. In August of 1914, at the outset of the First World War, the British and German armies fought at Mons in Belgium. The battle ended in a strategic retreat by the British, a demoralizing opening gambit to the war. Machen responded with a newspaper story that combined fiction and fact, imagining that angelic archers had appeared over the battlefield and fought alongside the British. This piece, "The Bowmen," soon caused mass confusion. Machen's previous stories for the paper had contained straight reporting, and the piece resembled other first-person accounts from soldiers frequently published in *The Evening News*. On top of this, censorship from the battlefield made it difficult for those at home to know exactly what had really taken place at the front. Many people believed that the story was true. Machen always maintained that it was fiction. Nevertheless, the story of the "the Angels of Mons" spread and became legendary, with soldiers confirming that they had seen the vision with their own eyes, and readers refusing to believe that Machen had made it all up.

The story was published in a collection of wartime fiction, which sold very well. Machen was encouraged to turn his attention back to creative writing, publishing a number of new stories. The relative financial security that he enjoyed at this point helped support a growing family. He and his wife had two children. But his career in journalism ended abruptly in a bizarre episode in 1921. That year he published an obituary of his former editor at *The Academy*, Lord Alfred Douglas. In the obituary he alluded to the homosexual affair between Lord Alfred and Oscar Wilde, which had been the cause of Wilde's trial and disgrace. Awkwardly for Machen, Lord Alfred was not, in fact, dead. He sued *The Evening News*. Machen was fired. He responded to his exile from Fleet Street with a quotation from the Psalms in Latin: "Eduxit me de lacu miseriae, et de luto faecis" ("He brought me up also out of an horrible pit, out of the miry clay," in the King James Version). One has to wonder whether he sabotaged his own career intentionally, or at least subconsciously.

Machen saw a resurgence in the popularity of his early fiction in the 1920s. His horror stories had been discovered in the United States. This led to a reappraisal of his work in Britain. He was frequently republished on both sides of the Atlantic throughout the decade. During the 1920s the Machens lived in St John's Wood where their house was the center of a literary salon and many parties. In the 1930s Arthur and Purefoy moved out of London, retiring to Amersham in Buckinghamshire, where they lived peacefully until Machen's death in 1947.

The importance of Arthur Machen and the range of his influence cannot be overestimated. Every significant writer of weird fiction in the twentieth century was influenced by him. H.P. Lovecraft considered him one of the very few "modern masters" of the genre. As a Christian thinker he had a profound influence on the Anglican mystic Evelyn Underhill. His book, *The Secret Glory*, read as a teenager, inspired the Christian faith of Sir John Betjeman.

"Here then is the pattern in my carpet," Machen once wrote, "the sense of the eternal mysteries, the eternal beauty hidden beneath the crust of common and commonplace things; hidden and yet burning and glowing continually if you care to look with purged eyes."

14
A Note on Flânerie

To walk, to meditate, to observe, to explore: these are simple but precious joys. The French have a certain type of man: the *flâneur*. This is translated as "stroller," "saunterer," or "lounger." The *flâneur* is a man who walks—not, like the *boulevardier*, to make an exhibition of himself—but aimlessly, with cultivated leisure and openness to his surroundings. Charles Baudelaire described the *flâneur* as a "gentleman stroller of city streets" and "botanist of the sidewalk."

Writers are often *flâneurs* because *flânerie*—the act of strolling—is such a useful stimulant to the creative mind. The great writers of the nineteenth century were all heroic pedestrians. Dickens walked fifteen miles per day. His nightly perambulations around London provided him with characters, scenes, and bits of dialogue for his books. He once set out at two o'clock in the morning and walked the thirty miles from London to his country home in Gad's Hill, Kent. Thomas De Quincey walked fifteen to twenty miles per day, in part to alleviate the effects of withdrawal from laudanum. Coleridge on occasion walked forty miles. Thomas Carlyle might have held the record at fifty four miles in a single day.

Many of these writers addressed *flânerie* in their works. *Sketches by Boz* consists in part of a long, lounging stroll across the length and breadth of London, as seen by Dickens. Arthur Machen wrote directly and thoughtfully on the subject. For Machen, *flânerie* was an almost mystical experience: the attentive *flâneur* could see *through* the landscape to the *genius loci*, and to the various intersections of life and history and imagination and place. "For if you think of it," Machen wrote, in *The London Adventure*, "there is a London *cognita* and a London *incognita*." In his 1923 memoir, *Things Near and Far*, Machen insists, "it is utterly true that he who cannot find wonder, mystery, awe, the sense of a new world and an undiscovered realm in the places by the Gray's Inn Road will never find these secrets elsewhere."

I love to walk. I walk everywhere. There are exceptions for practicality, of course. In the country I often bicycle. Over long distances I travel by train, plane, or boat. But I spend as little time as possible in automobiles. I think everyone would be happier if they walked more. The upheaval of our infrastructure, economy, and way of life to accommodate the automobile in the twentieth century was a tragic mistake.

15
Calvariae Disjecta

The following note appeared in the November 1883 issue of *The Folk-Lore Journal*: "At Burton Agnes Hall, East Yorks, there is a skull of a female, and, if it be buried out of the house, the whole place is disturbed with the most unaccountable noises, which last until it is brought into the Hall again: it now peacefully reposes in a closet in the wall."

Seven years later in 1890 a longer version of the story was published in *The Yorkshire Gazette*:

> Some years ago there was quite a stir in the neighbourhood of Burton Agnes Hall in the East Riding of Yorkshire, owing to the worthy Baronet who owns the property removing a skull, which had been in the home of the Boynton family from "the days whereof the memory of man runneth not to the contrary."
>
> The present Baronet, however, thought the skull had occupied its position long enough, and had frightened servants and page boys into fits for as many years as such a weird relic ought to do.
>
> Having thoroughly settled his mind on this point, he called to his gardeners and instructed them to remove the relic of [his] ancestors. They did so, and duly buried the skull in the garden.

Strange to relate, that no sooner was this done than dismal, unearthly noises were heard by night. The cries issuing in the vicinity of the skull were, in fact, fearful in their intensity; in the daytime, even after the burial of the relic, accidents of all kind took place, and everything in and about the hall went wrong.

The servants were simply frantic, and threatened to leave in a body. The more superstitious, in fact, had already left.

The remaining scion of the house of Boynton saw that unless he did something to appease the superstitious feelings of his household he would be left alone; so he made the best of a bad job and ordered his niece to replace the skull in its original resting place.

The relic was dug up, and consigned to a cupboard in the hall, right on the spot it formerly occupied, and by way of trial it was walled in. To this mode of procedure, the skull evidently had no objection, for peace has reigned in the hall ever since.

Calvariae Disjecta: The Many Hauntings of Burton Agnes Hall is a 2017 book edited by Robert Williams and Hilmar Schäfer that traces the development of a local legend through tellings and re-tellings since the nineteenth century. Beginning with the first mention of the skull in *The Folk-Lore Journal*, every article and book excerpt on the subject, up to the present day, is presented in chronological order. The reader is able to identify new details as they are added to the story. For example, in an account recorded by John Nicholson, in the 1890 book *The Folklore of East Yorkshire*, the ghost is given the name "Awd Nance" by servants at the hall.

The Elizabethan manor house at Burton Agnes was built between 1601 and 1610 by Sir Henry Griffith. The property has been in the same family since Roger de Stuteville settled there in 1173. When the male line died out it passed in the female line first to the Griffiths and later to the Boyntons and thence to the present owner.

The single most influential account of the Burton Agnes skull was a work of fiction. In 1893, Henry Frith, the English-language translator of Jules Verne's *Twenty Thousand Leagues Under the Sea* and *Around the World in Eighty Days*, wrote a series of thirteen ghost stories which were widely syndicated in regional newspapers under the collected title, "Haunted Ancestral Homes, Their Ghostly Visitors and Portents." The entry on "The Grinning Skull of Burton Agnes Hall" first appeared that year in *The Hampshire Telegraph*. It begins, "'Whither are you going, Anne?' asked Mistress Griffiths [sic] of her younger sister."

Anne Griffiths and her sister are presented by Frith as the daughters of Sir Henry Griffith, who built the hall. Frith portrays Anne as a contributor to the design of the house, to which she maintains a deep connection. "I would willingly die here," she says. "If my body could remain within its walls." One day on the road to Harpham, where she has been to visit friends, Anne is set upon by two beggars who rob her, beat her, and leave her for dead. She is carried back to Burton Agnes Hall where she makes her sisters promise that when she dies, "let my body be laid in the old churchyard, but let my head be separated from it and preserved within this house." However when she dies her sisters bury her body whole. The haunting then begins and continues until the corpse is dug up, decapitated, and the head brought home to the hall.

Frith's account is woven into nearly every re-telling of the story that follows. One of the figures in a painting of three women that hangs in the hall today has been identified by the family and tour guides as Anne Griffith. The website of Burton Agnes Hall names her as the ghost. But did Anne Griffith or Griffiths ever exist? Did Henry Frith base the details of his story on research, or was it simply an entertainment that he made up?

The answer appears later in *Calvariae Disjecta* in the form of an exhaustive study by Andy and David Clarke first published in 1996 in *Fortean Studies*. They write that, "research by English Heritage guide Margaret Imrie into the historical basis of the Griffith sisters has found no record of the existence of an ancestor called…Anne Griffiths [sic]." In the parish church "there is a memorial tablet, seemingly a copy of an earlier stone, which names three sons and two daughters of Sir Henry, but no

Anne." In the 1612 *Visitation of York* by the Norroy and Ulster King of Arms, "when Anne should have been noticed, only two Griffith children are recorded, these being Frances, aged 14, and Henry, aged 9—the only two known to have reached childhood." The authors point out that this would seem to "throw doubt on the painting" of the three women "dated 1620" since "only Frances appears to have survived childhood." The article ends with a tantalizing suggestion: "That the Griffith family were Welsh may be of significance in view of the Celtic predilection for skull guardians," the authors write. "Was a magical talisman needed to protect the newly constructed hall when the family moved to Yorkshire? And if so, who provided the skull?"

The pleasure of *Calvariae Disjecta* is to follow and untangle the threads of the original story as they are interwoven with fictions and strands of other related legends. Bettiscombe Manor in Dorset and Tunstead Farm in Derbyshire have screaming skulls of their own. *Calvariae Disjecta* means "skull fragments." It is an apt title. Williams and Schäfer are not interested in proving or disproving the narrative, only presenting the literary evidence. It would be nice to see other legends given similar treatment.

I enjoy ghost stories, but as a Christian I do not believe that the souls of the dead wander the earth. They are elsewhere, in trust to God, until that day when He throws open the tombs and raises the dead, knitting back together bodies and their souls, and restoring biological life to each and every person who has ever lived. Many hauntings are hoaxes, of course. Others have commonplace explanations. The real ones, I believe, are the work of nature-spirits, boggarts, and fairy folk.

16
Lord Tennyson in Camelot

Alfred, Lord Tennyson spent most of his career as a poet in the realm of Arthurian legend. It was not by any means his only subject, but it was one to which he returned again and again, and the one for which he is best remembered. His definitive treatment of the rise and fall of Camelot, the book-length cycle, *Idylls of the King*, was written over a quarter of a century between 1859 and 1885. But much earlier, at the outset of his career, Tennyson identified the unrealized potential in this iconic British mythology, writing that, "most of the big things except 'King Arthur' had been done."

Previous generations of Romantic poets had consciously rejected the subject. "As to Arthur...What have *we* to do with him," asked Coleridge. Lord Byron was likewise disinterested. "By the by," he wrote, "I fear that Sir Tristem and Sir Lancelot were no better than they should be...So much for chivalry. Burke need not have regretted that its days are over." Yet Tennyson dared to assert the relevancy of the Arthurian tradition to the modern world, and in so doing, achieved not only a masterpiece, but a renewal of the Victorian imagination.

Tennyson first read Sir Thomas Malory's fifteenth-century prose epic, *Le Morte d'Arthur*, in his youth. "The vision of Arthur as I have drawn him," he later told his son, "came upon me when, little more than a boy, I first lighted upon Malory." Tennyson understood the character as "a man who spent himself in the cause of honour, duty and self-sacrifice, who felt and aspired with his nobler knights, though with a stronger and clearer conscience than any of them."

It was not immediately clear to Tennyson how to approach the subject. In the 1830s he wrote four different poems that dealt with Arthur and Camelot in various ways. He also experimented with treatments and arrangements of the material in four outlines written during the same period.

The outlines were composed in the early 1830s, probably around 1833. The first describes the landscape of Camelot in prose, focusing on the mountain where Arthur's hall was built: "The Mount was the most beautiful in the world...but all underneath it was hollow, and the mountain trembled...and there ran a prophecy that the mountain and the city on some wild morning would topple into the abyss and be no more." The second outline records the symbolism that the young Tennyson attributed to various characters: the two Guineveres represent primitive Christianity versus Roman Catholicism; Mordred, the skeptical understanding; Merlin, science; the Round Table, liberal institutions; Excalibar, war. Another outline arranges the cast of characters based on their relationships to one another. The last is a proposed sequence for a five-act narrative connecting the legends. While none of these early sketches exactly predicted the form that Tennyson's mature work would take, they give a sense of the systematic approach he used to arrive at it.

The most famous of the poems from this period was *The Lady of Shalott*. It was based on a medieval Italian novelette from the thirteenth century collection, *Cento Novelle Antiche*. Tennyson was, at the time, unfamiliar with Malory's version of the tale and later said, "I doubt whether I should ever have put it in that shape if I had been then aware of the Maid of Astolat in *Mori Arthur*." The subtext in Tennyson's rendering is the movement of the artist from isolation and imitation of the world into experience of the world—in Tennyson's words, "out of the region of shadows into that of realities." To develop this theme, Tennyson modified the story substantially. Several important elements, like the Lady's mirror, are his invention, not present in the original source.

*Frontispiece (Illustration for Idylls of the King)
by Gustave Doré, 1878.*

The other three poems were *Sir Launcelot and Queen Guinevere*, *Sir Galahad*, and the *Morte d'Arthur*. In all of them Tennyson pays close attention to imagery, often expanding upon depictions in Malory's narrative for heightened emphasis. For example, he turns Malory's fairly straightforward image of Excalibur as a sword decorated with precious stones into a sword that "twinkled with diamond studs, / Myriads of topaz-lights, and jacinth-work / Of subtlest jewellery." But he also drew out and expanded the interior life of the characters. The dramatic last words that Tennyson gives to Arthur, while of his own invention, add to Malory rather than contradicting him. The emphasis of Arthur's speech in the *Morte d'Arthur* is on prayer; Arthur says, "More things are wrought by prayer / Than this world dreams of." The entire speech reflects Tennyson's skill at weaving his own moral vision into a poem that remains relatively faithful to the source material.

By the 1840s Tennyson had found in King Arthur a figure who could represent idealism and faith for Victorian society. His early experimentations would bear fruit in the *Idylls of the King*. In that work Tennyson navigated the knife's edge between the heroic and tragic, achieving something sublime. In the end Arthur slays the traitor Mordred in battle but is left "all but slain himself," his kingdom fallen. As in Malory, he is last seen taken by boat toward the mythical island of Avalon, "Somewhere far off, pass[ing] on and on, and go[ing] / From less to less and vanish[ing] into light." To cite Tennyson's own early symbolism: faith and virtue overcome materialism and doubt, but not without a cost. And indeed, the Victorian faith—*Tennyson's own faith*—was even then retreating into mysticism and agnosticism. But this was not a final retreat. Arthur is an inherently Christlike figure, destined to "come again / To rule once more." The *Idylls* end with another beginning: "And the new sun rose bringing the new year."

Writing about the Victorian period at the turn of the millennium, philosopher John Michell recalled,

> In my childhood some sixty years ago the code of behaviour one was supposed to live by was properly called Victorian. One source of that code was the Bible, and another was the romance of King Arthur. Putting them together, the Victorians conceived an ideal type of modern human being, the fair, kind, and honourable Christian gentleman.

> We have Tennyson in part to thank for that worthy ideal.

Epilogue
At Dennis Severs' House

I never had the chance to meet Dennis Severs but he was a man after my own heart. The architectural historian Gavin Stamp described him as "one of those Americans in England who seemed to have arrived from nowhere, to have no past, no roots and who, so irritatingly, could not be placed socially." I often suspect that my own London friends regard me similarly during the part of the year that I live there. Stamp wrote, "I first encountered him in the late 60s as the exotic friend of a Cambridge friend; he was then running horse-drawn open carriage tours around Hyde Park and the West End...and seemed, even for me then, a little too starry-eyed about the charm of Victorian England."

In 1979 Severs bought a Georgian terraced house at number 18 Folgate Street in Spitalfields, East London. Built around 1724 during the reign of King George I it was an exquisite but neglected property. The East End in those days was a slum. Stamp called it a "run-down, but mysterious, inner suburb." Instead of updating the house, Severs lived there without electricity or twentieth century technology. He would later recall,

> With a candle, a chamber pot and a bedroll, I began sleeping in each of the house's 10 rooms so that I might arouse my intuition in the quest for each room's soul.
>
> Then, having neared it, I worked inside out from there to create what turned out to be a collection of atmospheres: moods that harbour the light and the spirit of various ages in Time.

Severs created a fictional history for the house. It centered around the fictional Jervis family. They were prosperous Huguenot silk weavers whose fortunes waxed and waned during the course of the eighteenth and nineteenth centuries. Severs filled the house with period furniture and artifacts and devised complicated *tableaux* in each room. He opened the house to paying guests: his audience.

The tour that Severs conducted, beginning in the cellar and ending in the garret, reveals an elusive narrative. The museum's website explains:

> The game is that you interrupt a family of Huguenot silk weavers named Jervis who, though they can still sometimes be heard, seem always to be just out of sight. As you journey off into a silent search through the ten rooms, each lit by fire and candlelight, you receive a number of stimulations to your senses.
>
> It is the smell of food that first aligns your imagination with the faces around you in portraits. Then...Mr Jervis' wig, is it not the very same one that hangs over the back of his chair? His meal is only half eaten; did he abandon it when he heard us arrive?
>
> Visitors begin to do what they might if indeed they had travelled through a frame into a painting: use what they sense to piece together the scene they had missed. Thus (and this was Mr Severs' intention) what you imagine...is his art.

The experience is enchanting and often quite eerie. It is part theater, part art installation. The motto of the house is *Aut Visum Aut Non!*: "You either see it or you don't." But it is also someone's home—not Mr Jervis, but Mr Severs—who is simultaneously present and absent.

Before he died in 1999, Severs lamented that he had "come to accept" what he had "refused to accept for so long: that the house is only ephemeral. That no one can put a preservation order on atmosphere." Stamp concluded: "Certainly not now

Dennis Severs has gone to join the Jervises."

But recent history has unfolded differently than either man imagined. More than a decade later this strange museum/theater/gallery is still open to visitors. Under the curatorship of Severs's friend David Milne it is a thriving cultural landmark.

The narrative at 18 Folgate Street is not about the reign of Queen Victoria, *per se*. As one wanders through the rooms, and through time, one spends more of the silent tour in the eighteenth than the nineteenth century. But one emerges—yes, starry-eyed—into the Victorian period. It does not begin there, but ends there. Dennis Severs's House is one of those wonderful portals, of which London has many, through which a person can enter a lost world.

Sources

Chapter One:

Queen Victoria and the Arts

- Jones, Kathryn. (2012) "'To wed high art with mechanical skill': Prince Albert and the industry of art," in *Victoria & Albert: Art & Love, Essays from a study day held at the National Gallery*. https://www.royalcollection.org.uk/collection/themes/exhibitions/victoria-albert-art-love/the-queens-gallery-buckingham-palace/contents
- Kharibian, Leah. (2010) Passionate Patrons: Victoria & Albert and the Arts. London: Royal Collection.
- Marsden, Jonathan. (2010) Victoria & Albert: Art & Love. London: Royal Collection.
- Remington, Vanessa. (2012) "Queen Victoria, Prince Albert and their relations with artists," in *Victoria & Albert: Art & Love, Essays from a study day held at the National Gallery*. https://www.royalcollection.org.uk/collection/themes/exhibitions/victoria-albert-art-love/the-queens-gallery-buckingham-palace/contents

Chapter Two:

John Ruskin and the Arts

- Anthony, P.D. (1983) *John Ruskin's Labour: A Study of Ruskin's Social Theory*. Cambridge: Cambridge University

Press.

- Ruskin, John. (1866) *The Crown of Wild Olive: Three Lectures on Work, Traffic, and War.* New York: John Wiley & Son.
- Shrimpton, Nicholas. "Politics and economics," in O'Gorman, Francis (ed). (2015) *The Cambridge Companion to John Ruskin.* Cambridge: Cambridge University Press.

Chapter Three:

The Pre-Raphaelite Brotherhood

- Atterbury, Paul. (1995) *A.W.N. Pugin: Master of Gothic Revival.* New Haven: Yale University Press.
- Bartlett, Kenneth. (2013) *A Short History of the Italian Renaissaince.* Toronto: University of Toronto Press.
- Bronkhurst, Judith. (2006) *William Holman Hunt: A Catalogue Raisonné.* New Haven: Yale University Press.
- D'Arcens, Louise. (2016) *The Cambridge Companion to Medievalism.* Cambridge: Cambridge University Press.
- Dobbs, Brian; Dobbs, Judy. (1977) *Dante Gabriel Rossetti: an Alien Victorian.* London: Macdonald and Jane's.
- Doyle, Margaret. (2013) *Pre-Raphaelites: Victorian Art and Design, 1848-1900*, exhibition brochure. Washington, DC: National Gallery of Art.
- Fleming, Gordon. (1998) *John Everett Millais: A Biography.* London: Constable.
- Fowle, Frances. (2000) "Summary: Christ in the House of His Parents ('The Carpenter's Shop') 1849–50." http://www.tate.org.uk/art/artworks/millais-christ-in-the-house-of-his-parents-the-carpenters-shop-n03584.
- Gowing, Lawrence. (1983) *The Encyclopedia of Visual Art.* London: Encyclopedia Britannica International.
- Holman Hunt, William. (1905) *Pre-Raphaelitism and the Pre-Raphaelite Brotherhood.* New York: The Macmillan Company.
- Jacobi, Carol. (2012) "Sugar, Salt and Curdled Milk: Millais and the Synthetic Subject," Tate Papers 18. http://www.tate.org.uk/research/publications/tate-papers/18/sugar-salt-and-curdled-milk-millais-and-the-

synthetic-subject.
- Landow, George. (1979) *William Holman Hunt and Typological Symbolism*. New Haven: Yale University Press.
- Mancoff, Debra. (1990) *The Arthurian Revival in Victorian Art*. New York and London: Garland Publishing.
- Millais, John Guille. (1899) *The Life and Letters of Sir John Everett Millais*. London: Methuen & Co.
- Packer, Lona Mosk. (1963) *Christina Rossetti*. Berkeley: University of California Press.
- Prettejohn, Elizabeth (ed). (2012) *The Cambridge Companion to the Pre-Raphaelites*. Cambridge: Cambridge University Press.
- Rossetti, William Michael. (1895) *Dante Gabriel Rossetti: His Family-Letters with a Memoir*. London: Ellis and Elvey.
- Rossetti, William Michael. (1906) *Some Reminiscences of William Michael Rossetti*. New York: Charles Scribner's Sons.
- Rossetti, William Michael; Fredeman, William (ed). (1975) *The P.R.B. Journal: William Michael Rossetti's Diary of the Pre-Raphaelite Brotherhood, 1849-1853, Together with Other Pre-Raphaelite Documents*. Oxford: Clarendon Press.
- Ruskin, John. (1848) *Modern Painters*. London: Smith, Elder and Co.
- Ruskin, John. (1853) *The Stones of Venice, Volume the Second: The Sea Stories*. London: Smith, Elder, and Co.
- Tennyson, Alfred (Lord). (1906) *Juvenilia: and English Idyls*. London: Macmillan.
- Teukolsky, Rachel. (2009) *The Literate Eye: Victorian Art Writing and Modernist Aesthetics*. Oxford: Oxford University Press.
- Weintraub, Stanley. (1997) *Uncrowned King: The Life of Prince Albert*. New York: The Free Press.
- Willsdon, Clare. (2000) *Mural Painting in Britain 1840-1940*. Oxford: Oxford University Press.

Chapter Four:

Henry James and the Pre-Raphaelites

- Burne-Jones, Georgiana. (1906) *Memorials of Edward Burne-Jones.* New York and London: Macmillan.
- James, Henry. (June 20, 1869) "Letter to John La Farge." Manuscript. New York: The New-York Historical Society, La Farge Papers, ms 360.
- James, Henry. Lubbock, Percy (ed). (1920) *The Letters of Henry James.* New York: Charles Scribner's Sons.
- Rossetti, William Michael. (1895) *Dante Gabriel Rossetti: His Family-Letters with a Memoir.* London: Ellis and Elvey.

Chapter Five:

The Waterhouse Muse

- Baker, James K. Baker, Kathy L. (Fall 1999) "Miss Muriel Foster: The John William Waterhouse Model," in *The Journal of Pre-Raphaelite Studies.* New Series 8.
- Baker, James K. Baker, Kathy L. (2004) "The *Lamia* in the Art of John William Waterhouse," in *The British Art Journal.* Vol V, No 2.
- Rossetti, Dante Gabriel. Rossetti, William Michael (ed). (1895) *The Poetical Works of Dante Gabriel Rossetti.* London: Ellis and Elvey.
- Trippi, Peter. (2003) "John William Waterhouse," in *Pre-Raphaelite and Other Masters: The Andrew Lloyd Webber Collection.* London: The Royal Academy of Arts.
- Wood, Christopher. (1981) *The Pre-Raphaelites.* New York: The Viking Press.

Chapter Six:

Young England

- de Fonblanque, Edward Barrington. (1887) *Lives of the Lords Strangford.* London: Cassell, Petter, & Galpin.
- Faber, Richard. (1987) *Young England.* London: Faber and

Faber.

- Manners, Lord John James Robert. (1841) *England's Trust and Other Poems*. London: Francis & John Rivington.
- Michell, John. (2005) *Confessions of a Radical Traditionalist*. Waterbury Center [VT]: Dominion Press.
- Whibley, Charles. (1925) *Lord John Manners and His Friends*. Edinburgh: William Blackwood and Sons.

Chapter Seven:

A Ghost Story For Christmas

- Callow, Simon. (2012) *Charles Dickens and the Great Theatre of the World*. London: Harper Press.
- Dickens, Charles. (1836) *Sketches By Boz*. London: John Macrone.
- Dickens, Charles. (1837) *The Posthumous Papers of the Pickwick Club*. London: Chapman & Hall.
- Dickens, Charles. (1843) *A Christmas Carol*. London: Chapman & Hall.
- Forster, John. (1872-4) *The Life of Charles Dickens*. London: Chapman & Hall.
- Steele, Richard. (1887) *Isaac Bickerstaff, Physician and Astrologer*. London: Cassell & Company.

Chapter Eight:

Dickens and the Stage

- Callow, Simon. (2012) *Charles Dickens and the Great Theatre of the World*. London: Harper Press.
- Dickens, Charles; ed. Hartley, Jenny. (2012) *The Selected Letters of Charles Dickens*. Oxford: Oxford University Press.
- Kent, Charles. (1872) *Charles Dickens as a Reader*. Philadelphia: J.B. Lippincott & Co.

Chapter Nine:

An Account of Ye Olde Cheshire Cheese

- Dickens, Charles. (1859) *A Tale of Two Cities*. London: Chapman & Hall.
- Pennell, Joseph. (November 1887) "A Visit to Ye Olde Cheshire Cheese." *Harpers Weekly*.
- Reid, Thomas Wilson (ed). (1908) *The Book of the Cheese: Being Traits and Stores of 'Ye Olde Cheshire Cheese,' Wine Office Court, Fleet Street, London, E. C.* London: Privately Printed.

Chapter Ten:

The Last of the Coaching Inns

- Bruning, Ted. (2000) *Historic Inns of England*. London: Prion Books.
- De Quincey, Thomas. (1889-90) *The Collected Writings of Thomas De Quincey*. Edinburgh: A. and C. Black.
- Dickens, Charles. (1837) *The Posthumous Papers of the Pickwick Club*. London: Chapman & Hall.
- Jarvis, Robin. (2013) "Still Booking on De Quincey's Mail-Coach," *The Public Domain Review*. http://publicdomainreview.org/2013/02/20/still-booking-on-de-quinceys-mail-coach/
- Louras, Nick. (2016) *James Fenimore Cooper: A Life*. Winchester [UK]: John Hunt Publishing/Chronos Books.

Chapter Eleven:

Modern Origins of the Mystery Genre

- Collins, Wilkie. (1860) *The Woman in White*. London: Sampson Low, Son & Co.
- Collins, Wilkie. (1868) *The Moonstone*. London: Tinsley Brothers.
- De Quincey, Thomas. (1822) *Confessions of an English Opium-Eater*. London: Taylor and Hessey.

- Emrys, A.B. (2011) *Wilkie Collins, Vera Caspary and the Evolution of the Casebook Novel.* Jefferson [NC]: McFarland & Company.
- Kelly, Ruth. (1937) *The Influence of Thomas De Quincey on Edgar Allan Poe* (Unpublished master's thesis). University of Southern California, Los Angeles, California. http://digitallibrary.usc.edu/cdm/ref/collection/ p15799coll20/id/385613
- Doyle, Arthur Conan; Klinger, Leslie (ed). (2005-2006) *The New Annotated Sherlock Holmes.* New York: W.W. Norton.
- Purdon, James. (December 6, 2009) "The English Opium Eater by Robert Morrison," *The Guardian.* London. https://www.theguardian.com/books/2009/dec/06/ opium-eater-de-quincey-morrison
- Rzepka, Charles. "'A Deafining Menace in Tempestuous Uproars': De Quincey's 1856 *Confessions*, the Indian Mutiny, and the Response of Collins and Dickens," in Morrison, Robert (ed); Roberts, Daniel Sanjiv (ed). (2008) *Thomas De Quincey: New Theoretical and Critical Directions.* New York: Routledge.

Chapter Twelve:

The Symbolist Manifesto

- Butler, John Davis. (1967) *Jean Moréas: A Critique of his Poetry and Philosophy.* The Hague: Mouton.
- Moréas, Jean. (1889) *Les Premières armes du Symbolisme.* Paris: Léon Vanier.
- Thompson, Vance. (1913) *French Portraits.* New York: Mitchell Kennerley.
- Shryock, Richard. (March, 1998) "Reaction Within Symbolism: The Ecole Romane." *The French Review.* Vol. 71, No. 4.
- Wellek, René. (1967) "'Classical' Criticism in The Twentieth Century." *Yale French Studies.* No. 38.
- Nordau, Max Simon. (1895) *Degeneration.* New York: D. Appleton and Company.

Chapter Thirteen:

A Paean for Arthur Machen

- Anderson, Douglas A. (May 23, 2015) "Best Books," *Wormwoodiana*. http://wormwoodiana.blogspot.com/2015/05/best-books.html
- Hando, Fred. (1945) *The Pleasant Land of Gwent*. Newport: R H Johns Ltd.
- Lewis, D. B. Wyndham. (1944) *Take it to Bed*. London: Hutchinson & Co.
- Machen, Arthur. (1923) *The Works of Arthur Machen (Caerleon Edition)*. London: Martin Secker.
- Machen, Arthur. (1924) *The London Adventure, or The Art of Wandering*. London: Martin Secker.
- Machen, Arthur. (1988) *Selected Letters: The private writings of the Master of the Macabre*. Wellingborough: The Aquarian Press.
- Machen, Arthur; Sue Strong Hassler and Donald M. Hassler (ed). (1994) *Arthur Machen & Montgomery Evans: Letters of a Literary Friendship, 1923-1947*. Kent [OH]: The Kent State University Press.
- Sweetster, Wesley. (1964) *Arthur Machen*. New York: Twayne Publishers.
- Valentine, Mark. (1995) *Arthur Machen*. Bridgend: Seren Books.
- Wilson, A.N. (June 6, 2005) "Angels were on his side," *The Telegraph*. London. http://www.telegraph.co.uk/comment/personal-view/3617433/World-of-books.html
- "The Life of Arthur Machen." *The Friends of Arthur Machen*. http://www.arthurmachen.org.uk/machbiog.html
- "Arthur Machen's Writings: Annotated Bibliography." *The Friends of Arthur Machen*. http://www.arthurmachen.org.uk/machwork.html

Chapter Fourteen:

A Note on Flânerie

- Baudelaire, Charles, (1972) *Selected Writings on Art and Literature*. New York: Viking.
- Machen, Arthur. (1923) *The Works of Arthur Machen (Caerleon Edition)*. London: Martin Secker.
- Machen, Arthur. (1924) *The London Adventure, or The Art of Wandering*. London: Martin Secker.
- Machen, Arthur. (1992) *Ritual & Other Stories*. Carlton-in-Coverdale: Tartarus Press.

Chapter Fifteen:

Calvariae Disjecta

Baker, Phil. (April 26, 1017) "Skulduggery," *The Times Literary Supplement*. London.
https://www.the-tls.co.uk/articles/private/skulduggery-2/

- Williams, Robert (ed); Schäfer, Hilmar (ed). (2017) *Calvariae Disjecta: The Many Hauntings of Burton Agnes Hall*. Edinburgh: Information as Material.

Chapter Sixteen:

Lord Tennyson in Camelot

- Michell, John. (2005) *Confessions of a Radical Traditionalist*. Waterbury Center [VT]: Dominion Press.
- Tennyson, Alfred. (1859) *Idylls of the King*. London: Edward Moxon & Company.
- Tennyson, Alfred (Lord). (1906) *Juvenilia: and English Idyls*. London: Macmillan.

Epilogue:

At Dennis Severs' House

- Stamp, Gavin. (January 9, 2000) "Dennis Severs (Obituary)," *The Guardian*. London. https://www.theguardian.com/news/2000/jan/10/guardianobituaries
- "The Tour." *Dennis Severs's House.* https://www.dennissevershouse.co.uk/the-tour/

Index

About the Author

Nick Louras is a scholar of nineteenth century arts and letters. His essays appear in *The Baker Street Journal* and *Faunus: The Journal of the Friends of Arthur Machen*. His books include *James Fenimore Cooper: A Life*. He lives with his wife and three children in North Salem, New York and London, England.

CPSIA information can be obtained
at www.ICGtesting.com
Printed in the USA
BVHW041731220519
549027BV00007B/27/P